John Lydgate

THE TEMPLE OF GLAS

MIDDLE ENGLISH TEXTS SERIES

The Middle English Texts Series is designed for classroom use. Its goal is to make available to teachers and students texts that occupy an important place in the literary and cultural canon but have not been readily available in student editions. The series does not include those authors, such as Chaucer, Langland, or Malory, whose English works are normally in print in good student editions. The focus is, instead, upon Middle English literature adjacent to those authors that teachers need in compiling the syllabuses they wish to teach. The editions maintain the linguistic integrity of the original work but within the parameters of modern reading conventions. The texts are printed in the modern alphabet and follow the practices of modern capitalization, word formation, and punctuation. Manuscript abbreviations are silently expanded, and *u/v* and *j/i* spellings are regularized according to modern orthography. Yogh (ȝ) is transcribed as *g*, *gh*, *y*, or *s*, according to the sound in Modern English spelling to which it corresponds; thorn (þ) and eth (ð) are transcribed as *th*. Distinction between the second person pronoun and the definite article is made by spelling the one *thee* and the other *the*, and final *-e* that receives full syllabic value is accented (e.g., *charité*). Hard words, difficult phrases, and unusual idioms are glossed on the page, either in the right margin or at the foot of the page. Explanatory and textual notes appear at the end of the text, often along with a glossary. The editions include short introductions on the history of the work, its merits and points of topical interest, and brief working bibliographies.

John Lydgate
THE TEMPLE OF GLAS

Edited by
J. Allan Mitchell

Published for TEAMS
(The Consortium for the Teaching of the Middle Ages)
in Association with the University of Rochester

by

MEDIEVAL INSTITUTE PUBLICATIONS
Kalamazoo, Michigan
2007

Library of Congress Cataloging-in-Publication Data

Lydgate, John, 1370?-1451?
  The temple of glas / John Lydgate ; edited by J. Allan Mitchell.
    p. cm. -- (Middle English texts series)
  Text in Middle English; notes in English.
  "Published for TEAMS (The Consortium for the Teaching of the
Middle Ages) in association with the University of Rochester."
  Includes bibliographical references.
  ISBN-13: 978-1-58044-117-9 (pbk. : alk. paper)
  1. Venus (Roman deity)--Poetry.   I. Mitchell, J. Allan (John Allan),
1971- . II. Consortium for the Teaching of the Middle Ages.
III. Title.
PR2034.T4 2006
821'.2--dc22
                         2006028802

ISBN: 978-1-58044-117-9

CONTENTS

❧ ACKNOWLEDGMENTS

I am grateful to Russell Peck and John H. Chandler for their support and advice on this edition. Peter Brown, Nicky Hallet, and Thomas Crofts offered helpful suggestions. Melissa Furrow was extremely generous with the time she spent reading and commenting on the text, helping me to work out textual knots and saving me from some embarrassment. Any remaining faults are my own.

I also wish to thank the National Endowment for the Humanities for its generous support of the METS project, and Patricia Hollahan and the rest of the staff of Medieval Institute Publications for their work in helping to bring this volume out.

✤ INTRODUCTION

John Lydgate (c. 1371–1449) composed *The Temple of Glas* in the first quarter of the fifteenth century, though it is not certain for whom or what occasion, if any, the dream vision was written. Chaucer's *House of Fame*, written just around the time Lydgate was born, is usually recognized as one of the most important literary sources of inspiration for Lydgate. However, Lydgate does not consistently follow any single source or analogue but rather, in the style of a highly educated and capable medieval poet, absorbs and adapts materials from a cosmopolitan literary tradition to invent something new and enigmatic.

Lydgate belonged to the order of the great Benedictine abbey of Bury St Edmunds in Suffolk, and by the time he came to write *The Temple of Glas* he had already advanced through the stages of his novitiate to become an ordained priest. But he is not to be thought of as confined to a sheltered existence. Lydgate was sent to be educated at Oxford, and he spent stretches of time abroad and in London. Moreover, Bury St Edmunds was in some measure at the intersection of fifteenth-century political, intellectual, and religious life. In this milieu an aspiring poet could have found audiences hospitable to the type of fashionable courtly verse Lydgate produced in *The Temple of Glas*. Still, although the poem cannot be dated with any certainty, it may come from a period in the 1420s when Lydgate enjoyed comparative independence from the monastery.[1] For indeed, the poem is an example of secular court verse in which he indulged without the scruples one might assume (however anachronistically) in a medieval cleric. In fact, Lydgate took on multiple roles and worked in various genres throughout his career as a writer of love complaints, devotional verse, saints' legends, dramatic entertainments, historical works, didactic poems, satires, and more; and he responded to commissions from kings, clerics, guildsmen, and women of rank. The list of patrons "reads like a *Who's Who* of fifteenth-century England."[2] In effect, as James Simpson has observed, Lydgate's "corpus is riven by distinct, often exclusive, generic and discursive commitments."[3] Such is the long, retrospective view of a writer who put himself at the service not just of religion but also of the secular realm, and whose prolific literary output totals some 145,000 lines of verse to which it would be ludicrous to fasten a single label. When he wrote *The Temple of Glas* Lydgate was probably just beginning his career: the chronology is uncertain, but he had likely

---

[1] Pearsall, *John Lydgate* (1997), pp. 14 and 31.

[2] Edwards, "Lydgate Manuscripts," p. 21. Some contemporary humor might be found in an important early manuscript containing the *The Temple of Glas* copied by John Shirley (BL Add. 16165). In a prologue Shirley describes the black monk as a man who aimed to "plese gentyles," for which literary labor he was amply repaid: in what sounds like a pun (nobles = gentlemen and coins), Shirley says of Lydgate, "God wolde, of nobles he hade ful his hoode" (cited in *Lydgate's Temple of Glas*, ed. Schick, p. lxxxiii; transcribed in Connolly, *John Shirley*, pp. 206–08).

[3] Simpson, *Oxford English Literary History*, p. 52.

translated fables (e.g., *Churl and the Bird* and *Isopes Fabules*), composed other love poems (e.g., *A Complaynt of a Loveres Lyfe*), and attempted to render an extended French love allegory into English (*Reson and Sensuallyte*) — showing that his literary horizons were already expansive.[4]

The Temple of Glas takes the form of an elusive and suspenseful — but for that reason all the more sensational — dream vision that demands close attention to detail and the dynamic way in which the meaning of events unfolds. It also requires some detective work. Leaving aside complications generated by the framing fiction and the presence of the dreamer, the "plot" of the dream vision is deceptive in its simplicity. In it a lady is seen confessing to a secret desire for a man she is forbidden or unable to love but with whom, in the latter stages of the vision, she becomes joined in a cryptic extramarital ceremony conducted by Venus. The goddess instructs the couple to wait until some unspecified obstacle is removed, which will eventually allow them to consummate their love. What holds them back until then? Some readers have been inclined to take the poem as an allegory of adulterous love, the impediment to instant sexual gratification or a licit union being the lady's existing husband; but there may be some other, quite different set of constraints imposed on the couple by a guardian. The lady's dilemma may also be explained, in psychological terms, as a reluctance to yield the personal freedoms she recognizes are not available to women in public betrothal. Is she caught, like Criseyde in the second book of *Troilus and Criseyde*, between the desire for a romantic bond and fear of social institutions and coercive conventions that would transform romance into mere bondage? The anonymity and ambiguity of the affair prevents us from ascertaining such basic facts, the uncertainty of which is due as much to the narrative form of the work as to its matter. What may be called the limited legibility of the poem is a function of its fantasy structure.

A few critics have sought to plumb the mysteries by locating within *The Temple of Glas* a corresponding set of historical references and contemporary realia, proposing that Lydgate must originally have composed the poem to mark a public betrothal or clandestine marriage.[5] Encouragement for such literal readings of the poem can be found in a manuscript rubric written by John Shirley, a scribe who may have been personally acquainted with Lydgate: Shirley's early copy of the poem (BL Add. 16165) describes *The Temple of Glas* as "une soynge moult plesaunt fait a la request d'un amoreux par Lidegate Le Moygne de Bury" ("a very pleasant dream made at the request of a lover, by Lydgate the Monk of Bury").[6] Yet the statement is about as elliptical as the poem. For which lover might the poem have been commissioned? Over the years, various connubial and patronage arrangements have been conjectured and circumstantial evidence marshaled. Most recently it has been argued, based

---

[4] For comprehensive accounts of the poet's biography and bibliography, see Schirmer, *John Lydgate*; Pearsall, *John Lydgate* (1970); and more recently Pearsall, *John Lydgate* (1997).

[5] Critics usually assume adultery or marriage; the notion of a clandestine marriage was put forward by Kelly, *Love and Marriage*, pp. 291–93, and is accepted by Tinkle, *Medieval Venuses and Cupids*, pp. 154–59.

[6] See Connolly's *John Shirley*, the second chapter of which offers a discussion of BL Add. 16165; the likelihood of Shirley's personal acquaintance with Lydgate is addressed on p. 84. See also Edwards, "Lydgate Manuscripts," pp. 19–21, on the role of Shirley in disseminating Lydgate. Pearsall, *John Lydgate* (1997), p. 18, notes in general: "When Shirley tells us something in his rubrics, we may assume that it is not mere carelessness or desire to deceive, though he might embroider or exaggerate for effect or in order to assist in the construction of romantic narratives of the lives of the poets, or for the sake of enhancing his reputation as a communicator of inside knowledge."

on internal evidence such as the emblematic hawthorn (appearing in line 505 in one version of the poem) with its connections to the House of Lancaster, that Lydgate composed *The Temple of Glas* for the wedding of Henry IV and Joan of Navarre in 1403.[7] Other scholars propose later dates. That the motto of the lady in the dream (*De Mieulx en Mieulx*, line 310) is the same as that of the Paston family leads one early critic to wager that the poem was occasioned by the 1420 nuptials of William Paston and Agnes Berry.[8] Another believes the poem was begun in 1438 to celebrate the wedlock of Richard Roos and Margaret Vernon, though the same critic admits that *The Temple of Glas* equally appears to suit the marriage of Henry V and Katherine of Valois in 1420.[9] In this connection, however, with its strong suggestion of scandal and demands for secrecy, Lydgate's poem is more likely to be concerned with Queen Katherine's dalliances in the years following the death of Henry in 1422. For indeed, there is an argument to be made that Lydgate was lending his clerical authority and poetic craft to the cause of justifying the clandestine marriage of Katherine and Owen Tudor. Probably no later than the end of the decade the dowager queen had entered into wedlock with the Welsh squire, a union that had to be kept quiet both because it was morganatic and because it flouted a recent Act of Parliament (1427–28) that required an adult king to approve the widow's next marriage. Consequently, in the late 1420s the young queen was in a similar position to that of the lady in *The Temple of Glas*, unable publicly to exercise her "liberté" in affairs of the heart.[10] If in fact Lydgate's poem addresses Katherine's forbidden but not strictly speaking immoral (i.e., adulterous) affair, certainly

---

[7] Bianco, "New Perspectives," pp. 104–05, who proposes that the poem marked the 1403 royal union, at the same time acknowledges that *The Temple of Glas* may not have been all that suitable given its unsavory depiction of a sexually wayward Venus; see note 38 below.

[8] MacCracken, "Additional Light." Moore, "Patrons of Letters," pp. 193–94, soon gave excellent reasons to reject the idea that Lydgate was celebrating the wedlock of William and Agnes. Schirmer, *John Lydgate*, pp. 37–38, thinks the Pastons "improbable" but still believes the poem celebrated a wedding. William's son owned a copy of *The Temple of Glas* and once requested it urgently in interesting circumstances, on which see below.

[9] Seaton, *Sir Richard Roos*, pp. 375–76. The Prince of Wales, future Henry V, would go on to develop an important patronage relation with the poet: he commissioned *Troy Book* (c. 1412–20).

[10] On the amatory intrigues of Katherine see Griffiths, *Reign of King Henry VI*, pp. 60–62; Jones, "Catherine (1401–1437)"; and Strickland, *Lives of the Queens of England*, pp. 141–214. Katherine's earlier amorous attachment to Edmund Beaufort seems to have precipitated the parliamentary Act of 1427–28. Duke Humphrey of Gloucester would have been extremely put out had Katherine finally settled on Edmund, nephew to Gloucester's long-time rival Bishop Beaufort, who for his part must have stood to gain a great deal by promoting a royal marriage to one of his family members during the minority of Henry VI. Lydgate's relationship with Gloucester, whom the poet honors in other works from the same decade (e.g., *On Gloucester's Approaching Marriage*, written around 1422), makes it possible that *The Temple of Glas* takes the side of the Gloucester faction in opposing Beaufort by backing an alternative candidate in Owen. More detailed investigation is needed to decide whether the poem is about one or the other controversial love matches of the dowager queen, but at least the stealth involved in her marriage makes her a more likely candidate than the others proposed by scholars so far. Lydgate composed other poems for Katherine (on transience and in praise of the Virgin), and he celebrates her in several places; see Schirmer, *John Lydgate*, pp. 92, 106–07, 131–34, and 200, and Pearsall, *John Lydgate* (1970), pp. 164–65. Might she be the dedicatee at the end of *The Temple of Glas*?

we can more easily explain the monk's interest in the matter, and why it is said that the couple comes together "withoute synne" (line 1346).

But ultimately the list of candidates and corresponding dates — ranging from 1400 all the way to 1438 — may suggest that none of the particular historical occasions or individuals fits the poem satisfactorily, or exclusively. Attempts to pin down a single rationale for the poem also risk begging the question about which of the surviving versions is original or authorial (need there be only one?). I will return to these textual difficulties below. Still, some will find consolation in Shirley's assertion that the poem is a bespoke artifact — for the notion of a commission is, as Pearsall admits, "something to appease our sense of the preposterousness of a monk writing love-poems."[11] If Lydgate did write *The Temple of Glas* for a specific occasion the particular facts remain to be demonstrated. Like any good gossip the "facts" seem charged with significance, though their credibility and usefulness is uncertain.

One other possibility that needs to be considered is that a patron is just what Lydgate hoped to obtain with *The Temple of Glas*: the poem's notorious vagueness or abstractness may have been an attempt on the part of Lydgate, opportunist that he was, to attract the widest range of customers in different situations. There is indeed some circumstantial evidence that the poem had attracted several applications and audiences throughout the fifteenth century, for a point to which we will need to return is that the poem as we have it survives in three different versions, each of which may have been tailored ("customized") to fit different circumstances.[12] And in its afterlife the poem seems to have been employed in at least one other real-life romance:

> Sir John Paston demanded his copy in a hurry in 1461/2 when he was wooing Anne Haute; he probably wanted it, just as Slender wanted his "Book of Songs and Sonnets," to woo another Mistress Anne.[13]

But again the details are hazy and readers can only speculate as to their significance.

Seducing readers with possibilities remains what *The Temple of Glas* does best, and that special magnetism speaks not only to the provenance and textual history of Lydgate's poem but also to its literary qualities. For indeed, if *The Temple of Glas* appears to "go public" with private matters we can no longer identify, there is a way in which fresh documentary evidence (should it ever come to light) would not be enough to settle the text's meaning. Lydgate's poem is not reducible to the literal or referential level, for what it offers is a mystifying and alluring aesthetic experience.[14] Designed to seduce its audience with a spectacle of a secret and illicit love affair, *The Temple of Glas* is contrived to capture and concentrate attention. I will return to consider the implied or hypothetical audience of the work whose good favor

---

[11] Pearsall, *John Lydgate* (1970), p. 84.

[12] Bianco, "New Perspectives," p. 104.

[13] Seaton, *Sir Richard Roos*, p. 376. Sir John Paston was betrothed but never married to Anne Haute, though they were together for nine years and produced an illegitimate child, so the poem may have had particular poignancy in their case. See Davis, *Paston Letters and Papers*.

[14] Compare Bianco, "New Perspectives," p. 114, on the way the poem "demands critical engagement." Crockett, "Venus Unveiled," p. 68, also emphasizes the mysteries of the poem and compares the work to the detective novel: "The pleasure of reading a poem like *The Temple of Glas* may have been more like the pleasure of reading Arthur Conan Doyle than of reading Keats."

the poet attempts to court (i.e., "my lady," who is the poet's fictional paramour), but it may be equally important to recognize that the poem has designs on us (or any actual audience). Critics agree that it is charmingly obscure and faintly, delectably taboo. Something of the poem's sex appeal lies in the way it is curiously reticent and secretive about its purposes while remaining extremely suggestive, puzzling, provoking, even scandalous. How it manages to turn its relatively limited resources to advantage is worth considering. The following discussion attempts to highlight the "strategies of the text" around which the reader's aesthetic experience is structured and through which the meaning of *The Temple of Glas* is gradually realized.[15] Principally, these strategies include the careful modulation and juxtaposition of contrastive elements brought together in original and absorbing ways, making the poem itself a secret and seductive affair — which may, in fact, be the main point.

The Temple of Glas begins with the poet recalling how recently one December night he was kept awake by anxious and oppressive thoughts, the exact cause of which pensiveness is not identified. He tells us no more about his personal condition than that eventually he fell fast asleep and dreamt of being taken up to a resplendent Temple of Glass. Immediately the dream sequence recalls the opening to *The House of Fame* in which another disturbed dreamer is transported to a nearly identical location on a mid-December night. Explanatory notes to this edition will indicate the many debts Lydgate pays to Chaucer throughout *The Temple of Glas*, although tracking the intertextual references alone will not decode the poem. Long reputed for striving to imitate Chaucer, Lydgate has until recently been compared unfavorably with the older poet.[16] "The inevitable result," as Sue Bianco has said, "is that Lydgate, not being Chaucer, is found wanting."[17] In fact, Chaucer is only one point of departure for Lydgate: he owes much to Continental dream poetry and *dits amoureux* (e.g., *Le Roman de la rose* and Froissart's *Le Temple d'honneur*), and the results are post-Chaucerian due to substantive differences in execution and effect.[18]

While at one level *The Temple of Glas* clearly speaks to the legacy of Chaucer, it rapidly develops in other directions by absorbing and recombining "borrowed" elements. For example, the glassy temple and its icy foundation (lines 16–20) are details picked up directly from different places in *The House of Fame* but coupled together here in order to lay special em-

---

[15] The terminology is that of Iser, *Act of Reading*.

[16] For example, Schirmer, *John Lydgate*, p. 38, criticizes the poet for being "imitative" and "remote from life in his archaic book-knowledge and predilection for rhetoric." Norton-Smith, "Lydgate's Changes," p. 177, says the "borrowings of time and place illustrate Lydgate's characteristic stripping away of Chaucerian complexity, especially of allegory." For Spearing, *Medieval Dream-Poetry*, p. 173, the poem indicates Lydgate's "failure to grasp what is really happening in fourteenth-century dream-poems." And Russell, *English Dream Vision*, pp. 199–201, agrees that Lydgate pays homage to his elder without coming close to rivaling his achievements. New approaches to Lydgate do not find much use for these tired truisms, and Edwards, "Lydgate Scholarship," confirms that actually they have long been suspect. Simpson, *Oxford English Literary History*, p. 50, offers a salutary corrective: "almost none of Lydgate's works is directly imitative of Chaucer: those poems that do relate to Chaucer's do so with more powerful strategies in mind than slavish imitation."

[17] Bianco, "New Perspectives," p. 96.

[18] On the French background, see, for example, Bianco, "Black Monk," and Boffey, "English Dream Poems"; and for examples in translation, see Windeatt, *Chaucer's Dream Poetry*.

phasis on the symbolism of the Temple of Glass.[19] Lydgate's dedicated focus on the lovers' shrine is distinctive. Remaining for the duration in and around the precincts of the building (rather than treating it as a picturesque diversion en route to the House of Fame as in Chaucer), Lydgate finds scope for his own poetical invention by moving *through* Chaucerian images. Not content with superficial appearances, the poet investigates the depths of the temple. As if extending and dilating upon a brief moment in Chaucer's *House of Fame*, Lydgate makes something original and strangely — if only deceptively — familiar.

The scenes inside the temple confirm the poet's own conscious preoccupation with mutability and superficiality; surface appearance is a main theme. Having entered the place through a small "wiket" (line 39), resembling portals found in French love allegories as well as in Chaucer's *House of Fame* and Merchant's Tale, the dreamer goes on to describe what he saw on the walls. They depict "sondri lovers" (line 46), both faithful and faithless, divine and human, married and adulterous, grouped together according to no self-evident organizing principle. Many of the famous lovers are derived from Ovid's *Metamorphoses* but also appear prominently in Chaucer's works. Seth Lerer has thus argued that Lydgate is here emulating a Chaucerian anthology: the wall painting, with its précis of The Knight's Tale in the center and of The Squire's Tale at its end, functions as a tribute and table of contents to Chaucer's works in the manner of the catalogue in the F-Prologue to *The Legend of Good Women*. For Lerer, this apparent homage to the older poet is symptomatic of the younger poet's anxious fixation on Chaucer's paternal authority. But there is surely also something unsettling about Lydgate's casual listing of the images displayed on the walls, making it hard to accept that they could be so transparent (even if made of glass). They do more than just mediate Chaucer. For indeed, "various traditions merge and combine" on the walls.[20] Lydgate treats literary tradition here as though it were itself in a state of flux. That volatility about the place is made emphatic in the image of Venus — herself portrayed floating on the sea, the focal but fluid image around which lovers gather to present their pleas (lines 50–54), while also appearing several lines later as one of the lovers (lines 126–28). Multiform and mutable throughout, Venus will figure later in *The Temple of Glas* as a statue, a planet, and an active deity.[21] Her variable ontology matches the metamorphoses and miscellaneousness of the lovers on the temple mural and indicates the freedom with which the poet felt he could combine disparate materials.

The dreamer goes on to report that the sanctuary of the temple is crowded with thousands of people who have come to present appeals to Venus (lines 143–246). Here the poem comes to resemble other near-contemporary love allegories, such as *The Assembly of Ladies* and *Kingis Quair*, which feature courts of love where pleas are presented and adjudicated.[22]

---

[19] Spearing, *Medieval Dream-Poetry*, p. 173, argues that Lydgate takes up such details because he is "interested in such things simply for their own sake, as a magpie is attracted by anything shiny." Yet comparable images of mutability, fragility, and flux have an important place in *The Temple of Glas*, as befits a poem about shifting loyalties and erotic passions (especially if they are unsanctioned).

[20] See Pearsall, *John Lydgate* (1970), pp. 39–40, who notes that some figures (e.g., Theseus and Canacee and her brother) appear in the list for reasons that have nothing to do with love.

[21] See Bianco, "New Perspectives," pp. 109–14; and Tinkle, *Medieval Venuses and Cupids*, pp. 129–35. But Schick, in his edition of *Lydgate's Temple of Glas*, p. cxxxvi, complains that this is evidence of the poet's confusion ("general muddle-patedness").

[22] The relationships between *The Temple of Glas* and literary and historical "courts of love" is explored by Boffey, "'Forto compleyne.'"

The diverse amatory predicaments of the lovers mirror the sorrowful conditions depicted on the walls (i.e., unrequited love, jealousy, duplicity, absence, abandonment, the incompatibility of youth and age, the interference of parents), though some lovers face the further and perhaps "present-day" impediments of forced religious celibacy and arranged marriages. One does not have to read far into *The Temple of Glas*, then, to realize that the poem is a frank exposé of the refractory desires which lurk behind the masks of social propriety and conscience, even escaping the most cherished legal and moral bonds. The antithesis between spontaneous sexual passion and imposed social controls, or between desire and duty, begins to emerge as another preoccupation of Lydgate's *The Temple of Glas*.[23] And it is one more sign of the poet's concern with what lies under surfaces and simulacra.

It may seem significant, indeed, that the poet goes so far as to peer under the cloak of his religion. Here Lydgate imagines one group of female complainants, committed at a young age to the convent by their parents and now unable to renounce their vocation, who "al her life cannot but complein, / In wide copis perfeccion to feine" (lines 203–04). Some critics are tempted to think Lydgate is getting personal, as though the passage were a "belated *cri de coeur* for what he has missed."[24] Lydgate was himself only a boy when he joined the order at Bury.[25] The passage is clearly sympathetic, even if not symptomatic of his own repressed desire; certainly there is no overt moral condemnation of the hypocrisy of holy women who conceal sexual love-longing. But the complaint, however moving or relevant, is conventionally grouped together with others, and it refers to a practice that was obsolescent by the fifteenth century.[26]

A more likely scenario is that Lydgate presents himself as the opposite sort of fellow, adopting the "Chaucerian stance of noncombatant,"[27] claiming no experience of love, for it does not seem that he has come to Venus' temple for amatory reasons. Yet this Chaucerian stance, as we will see, may just be a momentary disguise or self-delusion.[28] After describing the temple building and the multitude of lovers within, the dreamer fixes a loving gaze on one female supplicant whom he saw kneeling beside the statues of Pallas and Venus. In a conventional but highly focused description of the physical and personal attributes of the courtly lady (lines 250–320), the dreamer perceives that she is a paragon of beauty, courtesy, discretion, and faithfulness. He is like another Troilus struck by Criseyde in the Palladian

---

[23] Compare Tinkle, *Medieval Venuses and Cupids*, pp. 154–59.

[24] Pearsall, *John Lydgate* (1970), p. 104. The idea was originally expressed in *Lydgate's Temple of Glas*, ed. Schick, pp. lxxxviii and cxiii. Spearing, *Medieval Dream-Poetry*, p. 174, thinks the poetry here is especially good because it draws on something at least closer to personal experience than romantic love.

[25] Pearsall, *John Lydgate* (1997), p. 13.

[26] For similar complaints in Middle English poetry, see *Court of Love*, lines 1095–1136, and James I's *Kingis Quair*, lines 624–30. On the practice of "child oblation" and its decline in the later medieval period, see de Jong, *In Samuel's Image*, pp. 44–45, 294, 297, et passim. Readers can be forgiven for speculating about a monk who gives expression to wayward sexual desire in agreeable verse. Often mentioned but seldom discussed, the paradox of a celibate cleric indulging in romantic fantasies exerts an irresistible tug. There are other examples (e.g., Douglas, Dunbar, Skelton) of celibate love poets, and Lydgate may have been writing for commission or even "on spec." Still, Lydgate's autobiographical questions (long out of favor in modern literary scholarship) will not go away.

[27] The phrase is from Lawton, "Dullness and the Fifteenth Century," p. 767.

[28] Appearing to do things like Chaucer is indeed one of the ways Lydgate may be able to "get away" with artistic choices he would otherwise need to justify.

temple. Yet it is not explained how, just by looking at the lady, the dreamer could have gauged not just her appearance but the quality of her character or "condicioun" (line 284). His penetrating, voyeuristic gaze is an important part of the fantasy, a fictional world of his own invention (or projection) in which surfaces and depths unexpectedly converge. Sight and seduction are intimately related on the diegetic level of *The Temple of Glas*, the piercing look functioning throughout as a leitmotif describing the eyes of the beloved whose rays reach deep into the heart (e.g., lines 262–63, 582–83, 813–17).[29] Sight violates normal boundaries, upsets the order of things, and is not merely a passive faculty. The dream vision, as it develops, is itself invasive: the dreamer exposes private affairs, secret rites, intimate hopes and fears, in an act of looking that is really a kind of longing.[30] Moreover, his looks are invested with a fetishistic desire comparable to that of the lovers. Indeed the poet's experiences will seem to develop into those of a Chaucerian combatant unexpectedly engaged in love. Narration, as we can already discern in this early part of the poem, becomes an act of adoration.

But if the dreamer seems to unveil everything, important elements remain unknown and untold. Who, for example, is the lady? Her clothing is green and white, decorated with scrolls, and emblazoned with the motto *De Mieulx en Mieulx* (line 310), as though she were some specific and identifiable person. The dreamer goes on to report her complaint to Venus, inviting further speculation about her identity:

For I am bounde to thing that I nold,	*don't want*
Freli to chese there lak I liberté.	*where*
And so I want of that myn herte would —	*lack; desires*
The bodi knyt, althoughe my thought be fre —	*tied*
So that I most of necessité	*must*
Myn hertis lust outward contrarie;	*outwardly contradict*
Thogh we be on, the dede most varie.	*one (united); deed*
Mi worship sauf, I faile eleccioun;	*honor preserved*
Again al right, bothe of God and Kynd,	*Against*
There to be knit undir subjeccion . . . (lines 335–44)	

Her complaint, candid though it may seem, is short on specifics. The evocative language she uses to describe her double bind suggests that the lady may be caught in a loveless marriage, betrothed to be married against her will, or prevented from marrying at all due to a religious vow or some other regulation. At this point the reader is left guessing. It is only clear that she desires a man she cannot possess:

For he that hath myn herte feithfulli	
And hole my luf in al honesti	*completely [possesses]*
Withoute chaunge, albeit secreli,	
I have no space with him forto be. (lines 363–66)	

---

[29] Compare Miskimin, "Patterns in *The Kingis Quair* and the *Temple of Glas*," p. 354.

[30] For an intelligent discussion of looking and longing in other poems besides *The Temple of Glas*, see Spearing's *Medieval Poet as Voyeur*.

In reply, Venus promises that some day the lady will have what she desires, though she must wait patiently, and that meanwhile the man will be made to love her devotedly (lines 370–453). The lady then praises the goddess for her beneficence (lines 461–502). Venus bestows on her a green and white hawthorn chaplet along with instructions about constancy in love (lines 503–23). The first part of the poem ends with great promise.

The second part opens with the dreamer leaving the commotion of the temple to be alone, whereupon he sees a solitary man complaining (lines 567–693), thus recalling Chaucer's encounter with the grief-stricken knight in the *Book of the Duchess*. But Lydgate's man is lamenting his subjection to the God of Love. He has just now been smitten by the sight of a lady in the temple (fulfilling Venus' promise at lines 440–53) and finds himself suspended between dread and hope. And he is unaware of being observed by the dreamer. The parallel with *Book of the Duchess* lies not in the details of the man's situation but rather in the distancing effect produced by the presence of a naïve or uncomprehending dreamer: for at this stage the dreamer does not or cannot say if the object of the man's affection, whom the man calls "goodli fressh in the tempil yonder" (line 577), is the same lady who featured in the first part and was described as "so goodli on to se" (line 269). The lover's own stereotyped description of the lady hardly narrows down the possibilities, for every courtly lady is superlatively excellent. He does not mention her motto or any other distinguishing marks; and he shows no cognizance of the practical obstacles she raised in her earlier speech to Venus, for in his lament the man thinks the only thing keeping him from her is his own dread and her "Daunger" ("Aloofness" — line 646). If she is married or otherwise "knit undir subjeccion" (line 344), then ironically he faces additional obstacles. The dreamer does not seem any better informed, or at least we can say he is hardly informative on this point. Lydgate's practice of postponing the truth and merely teasing out implications — all the while seeming to expose everything — generates subtle ironies and mounting tensions.

The man goes on to make his own complaint to Venus (lines 701–847), pleading for Cupid to strike the lady with his firebrand so that she becomes enflamed with passion. But if she is the same lady, then why should he have to ask? It has been suggested that the man's complaint about unrequited love is "rather ungrateful, and Venus's promise of help unnecessary."[31] Probably the lover does not know as much as Pearsall thinks he should, and it is right to recall that the lady loves him "albeit secreli" (line 365). Here we must recognize that the lady enjoys an uncommon autonomy and priority in the narrative of events — and that the man's perspective is particularly incomplete and his understanding belated.[32] Lydgate is managing a narrative of self-discovery and disclosure for the male lover as for the narrator and the reader, presenting events in an allegory that compresses time and space for poetic effect. Part of reading *The Temple of Glas* is learning how to read.

Venus subsequently tells the man to take heart and speak to the lady, for "Withoute spech thou maist no merci have" (line 912). Once he gathers his courage (and the poet collects his wits to be able to relate what happens next), the man goes on to address the lady, asking for mercy and promising fidelity and secrecy (lines 970–1039). She grants him her love as far as she is able, telling him that until Venus "list provyde / To shape a wai for oure hertis ease" (lines 1082–83), they must wait. The reader must also wait to see whether these vague references will be clarified; for now, at least, given the lady's reference to her own dif-

---

[31] Pearsall, *John Lydgate* (1970), p. 108.

[32] Scanlon, "Lydgate's Poetics," pp. 86-90.

ficulties, we can be quite certain that she is the same one who approached Venus earlier. The love allegory thus advances by incremental steps, gradually revealing its perturbed meanings; the reader's understanding is cumulative, albeit uncertain.

Venus now embraces the pair in a golden chain and, in a lengthy hortatory speech that is pivotal within the whole sequence of the dream, she instructs the pair of lovers: the couple must remain truthful, humble, and courteous until the day of their deliverance (lines 1106–1277). And the lovers are told that the waiting is for their own good: "So thee to preve, thou ert put in delay" (line 1193). The idea that something becomes more precious the harder it is to attain is central to the whole experience of the poem, not only for the lovers but also for readers. Here the principle is elucidated at some length: Venus lays out what is known as the doctrine of contraries (lines 1250–63), derived originally from Boethius' *Consolation of Philosophy* and later twisted into its present form by Chaucer's Pandarus in *Troilus and Criseyde*. But Venus' speech is not only informative, elucidating a philosophical point about the benefits of long-suffering for committed lovers; her speech is also "performative," in the sense that it sanctions and secures their commitment. In a quasi-nuptial procedure — as if officiating at a marriage ceremony before the whole temple — the goddess has the couple hold hands, make vows, and finally kiss. She then locks their hearts with a golden key (line 1225), and at the same time Venus proclaims the couple is united: "Eternalli, be bonde of assuraunce, / The cnott is knytt, which mai not ben unbound" (lines 1229–30). As mentioned, this central legislative act has itself become something of an interpretive knot that will not come undone, despite great scholarly ingenuity.[33]

The dreamer is now nearing the end of his vision. When Venus finishes her exhortation to the lovers, the temple rings out with praise, the Muses sing, Orpheus and Amphion harp, and lovers pray to the goddess. Venus provides further assurances, and the whole temple joins in a ballade glorifying Venus who has "withoute synne / This man fortuned his ladi forto wynne" (lines 1346–47; compare 450). Venus' determination to keep the lovers from committing sin has led some critics to suppose that Lydgate has, so to speak, baptized Venus. In this reluctance to allow the couple immediate gratification, the poet has been accused by some of exerting the pressure of his monkish morality after all. Schick comments that in Venus' speeches she "occasionally appears to us in a very philistine aspect."[34] C. S. Lewis says the poet's punctiliousness in this regard makes his conception of love more "modern" than in previous medieval poems — since being married "had not troubled Guinevere."[35] Pearsall says the "presence of Venus is didactic" and her scruples are a way for Lydgate to avoid the embarrassment of promoting an extramarital union.[36] Anna Torti argues that Venus comes increasingly to act as a force of social order and is a proponent of Christian values.[37] Yet if the majority of critics are also right about the nature of the relationship (i.e., extramarital), then Venus' unorthodox commitment ceremony may be taken to be sanctioning non-normative, patently sinful sexual desire anyway: she would be paying no heed to the biblical idea of adultery "in the heart" (see Matthew 5:27–28). There are reasons to believe Venus' "cnott

---

[33] Compare Bianco, "New Perspectives," p. 114.

[34] *Lydgate's Temple of Glas*, ed. Schick, p. cxxxv.

[35] Lewis, *Allegory of Love*, p. 241.

[36] Pearsall, *John Lydgate* (1970), pp. 106–07.

[37] Torti, *Glass of Form*, pp. 77–80.

. . . which mai not ben unbound" may itself point to the ignominy of adultery rather than to the marriage bond.[38] Arguably, then, her reasons for self-restraint and fortitude may be no less pragmatic than those of Pandarus (e.g., *Troilus and Criseyde* 1.953–61), rather than the principled expression of Christian morality. Perhaps Venus may be counted on for being even more treacherous behind the scenes than Chaucer's go-between ever was in *Troilus and Criseyde*, for as Lewis suggests the goddess may be euphemistically vowing that "something may happen" to the unwanted husband, so that the couple need not wait very long before they are finally able to be together.[39] One is reminded here of such drastic measures as the fatal "furie infernal" sent by the gods as a kind of *deus ex machina* in Chaucer's Knight's Tale: a rivalry between lovers is there resolved only by the untimely death of one of them. Palamon consequently wins Emelye, and he, it will be remembered, was a knight of Venus.

To return to the scholarly search for historical referents and nuptial occasions, it would be surprising to discover that the poem had ever celebrated a straightforward conjugal arrangement. On the one hand, it would be in bad taste for Lydgate to leave any hint that the female partner was adulterous, rebellious, or devious. On the other, the terrible pathos of the lady's situation leaves readers with little to celebrate. At this point an argument could be made that *The Temple of Glas* is closer to being anti-matrimonial (whether ironically so or not), in conformity with the nature of the goddess of unregulated sexual passion, i.e., Venus. This reading may seem unlikely for Lydgate, the monk, until one considers the way extramarital love has already been glamorized in Tristram and Isolde (lines 77–79), Paris and Helen (lines 92–93), and Mars and Venus (lines 126–28). While there are also references to faithful wives (e.g., lines 405–10), the romantic discourse running throughout the work is that artificial social constraints such as marriage are worthy only insofar as they do not oppress the natural passions and free choice; duty is subordinate to desire. Venus' logic of contraries perhaps embodies the rationale of the work ("For white is whitter if it be set bi blak," line 1250), the substance of which logic could be set out schematically: forced or loveless marriage is bad; therefore, extramarital affection is good.[40] The consensual nature of the second kind of relationship trumps the austere legality of the first. Far from being epithalamic, then, *The Temple of Glas* may constitute a genuine counter-discourse and social critique in its defiance of "compulsory conjugality."[41] Is not this poem about love and its liberation (e.g., lines 209–14)? By the same token, the poem has also been read as an "ironic allegory" of the sinful excesses of sexual immorality.[42] There is, perhaps, a melancholy and

---

[38] Bianco, "New Perspectives," p. 111, notes that the love knot may be unpropitious: "When she binds the lovers together . . . is she performing a 'marriage' ceremony, or simply echoing the action of Vulcan in the early part of the poem?" Compare Crockett, "Venus Unveiled," p. 85, who argues that the chain of Venus is an "image of enslavement to erotic love."

[39] Lewis, *Allegory of Love*, p. 242.

[40] Why might Lydgate come at the topic in this indirect manner? He may have polarized the issue between social constraint and individual consent to make it palatable. The antithetical frame of mind is something for which the poet has been criticized by Pearsall, *John Lydgate* (1970), pp. 110–15, but it allows him some immunity by stirring up pathos for ideas that would otherwise be too easy to discountenance.

[41] The phrase is from Walker, "Muse of Indifference," p. 204.

[42] Crocket, "Venus Unveiled," argues that in *The Temple of Glas* Lydgate employs "ironic allegory" (p. 69) to condemn the idolatry and sensuality of the lovers and all that Venus symbolizes.

ultimately monkish recognition of the "wo that is in marriage" (Wife of Bath, *Canterbury Tales* III [D], 3).

Could the poem ever constitute a flattering epithalamium? Perhaps the only occasion in which the poem would seem appropriate as matrimonial verse is if it were read in relation to a clandestine wedding, such as the one that took place between Katherine and Owen, as mentioned above. In such a difficult circumstance the lady could come off as courageous rather than false, and the monk would be pressing a case for the recognition of true married love over against the interdictions of the state. We cannot rule out nuptials such as these.

The epilogue to the poem opens up further questions. The heavenly hymn sung in the temple causes the dreamer to start up from his slumber, and he is immediately grief-stricken for lack of the happy vision (lines 1362–66). But whereas he went to bed oppressed by some vague anxiety, now his sorrow has a specific object:

gret thought and wo	
I hade in hert and nyst what was to do,	*knew not*
For hevynes that I hade lost the sight	
Of hir that I all the longe nyght	
Had dremed of in myn avisioun.	*dream vision*
Whereof I made gret lamentacioun	
Bicause I had never in my life aforne	*previously*
Sein none so faire, fro time that I was borne . . . (lines 1370–77)	

The poet has ended up like the man in the dream, struck by the "sight" of the lady in the temple, but not yet assured of a requital. But there may be some considerable perversity to the poet's situation compared to that of the man: not only has he dreamed the whole thing up, but he also is smitten by an unavailable woman. Or is there some other naughty secret? Perhaps the man in the dream is really a surrogate for the dreamer himself.[43]

Reminiscent of Chaucer when he apologizes at the end of *Troilus and Criseyde*, the poet finally vows to write a little treatise in praise of women; and then he dedicates his book to "my lady." The reader is left speculating, again, about what all this means. Has the poet discovered love through the dream? Or, is the dream a wish-fulfilment fantasy relating to a prior affair? Is his paramour merely dreamt up, or does she have a real existence outside the text? Is she the poet's female patron cast flatteringly as a beloved? And what might she find enchanting in the work?

The poet registers some uncertainty himself about the nature of the dream and requires "leiser" to "expoune my forseid visioun, / And tel in plein the significaunce, / . . . So that herafter my lady may it loke" (lines 1388–92). Davidoff suggests the import of the dream has been fulfilled already in the poet's desire to communicate with the lady: by writing to her he is putting into practice Venus' advice to the male protagonist: "For specheles nothing maist thou spede" (line 905).[44] But if so, the speech he has chosen to make (i.e., the poem) is encrypted. In the concluding lines, in a variation on a favorite Chaucerian envoy, the poet sends off his work to an unnamed beloved, "I mene that benygne and goodli of hir face"

---

[43] Compare Torti, *Glass of Form*, pp. 81–82; Davidoff, *Beginning Well*, p. 141. An older view has it that the dreamer is "merely an observer" before whom a dream unfolds without involving him in interesting (i.e., Chaucerian) ways; see Spearing, *Medieval Dream-Poetry*, p. 174.

[44] Davidoff, *Beginning Well*, pp. 144–45.

(line 1402), employing words used earlier by the man inside the dream to describe the lady. The poem invites us to make such connections, however tenuous, between the vision and the framing fiction, as is typical of Middle English dream visions. They are not as a rule mere flights of fancy: "the dream world is not to be thought of as wholly different from waking experience, but in some measure a different account of it, although the connections are not always immediately obvious."[45] Indeed so much remains unknown.

Looking back it is clear that Lydgate employs specific strategies to solicit desire, courting not only "my lady" but also a wider audience: the poem seduces by being full of promises and portents that describe everything without precisely explaining anything. The point can be illustrated with the distinction between the *story* and the *discourse*.[46] On the level of the story (i.e., narrated events occurring within the dream) desire is articulated and aroused in the sentimental speeches of the lovers when they address the goddess and each other. But even as the lovers appear to be confessing their innermost feelings, their mannered speeches make it difficult to tell exactly what they are saying or doing — so complete is the exposure of their private sentiments, their practical lives remain concealed. Who are these anonymous apparitions? What exactly is the obstacle that separates them from each other? Spectral figures in a dream, the secret lovers resist even as they invite identification. Something of the erotic energy of the dream vision clearly resides in a frustrated form of desire that is the result of carefully modulated obfuscation and illumination, concealment and exposure — or what Roland Barthes calls "intermittence."[47] On the level of the poetic *discourse* (i.e., the narration of the dream) the poet finds himself drawn in and increasingly engaged: he emerges at the end with a burning desire to communicate with the lady of the dream. Attracted by her sexy figure, he becomes her devoted lover and poet. But the dreamer is himself a phantom figure, a fiction, a nameless conduit. The dream is not just a vision of lovers; the poet envisages himself. How is this figure related to *the* poet? Why is Lydgate, a monk, mediating such experiences? Whence this strange telepathy? And who is "my lady" but another specter of desire? *The Temple of Glas* effectively becomes an elaborate love letter, a sort of Valentine intended to work its charms on some unknown other.

Taken together, the trajectories and circuits of erotic energy traced by these questions indicate something of the multiple, mutable, and equivocal nature of desire in *The Temple of Glas*. And posterity can hardly escape the pull of its articulate eroticism, or what can be identified as the affective dimension of the work. The dream lady, for one thing, seems to have provoked readers from very early on. Comments found in the margins of the poem in one late fifteenth-century manuscript (MS Bodley 638) are indicative: alongside passages referring to the lady at line 847 (fol. 29v) there is a quizzical remark, *hic vsque nescio quis* ("up to this point I do not know who"); and at line 972 (fol. 31v) there is an apparently exasperated marginal comment, "who in all godly pity maye be," the impatience of which is perhaps reinforced by the use of the vernacular rather than Latin.[48] As observed already, the poem makes sense cumulatively ("up to this point") but not completely and conclusively.

---

[45] Brown, *Reading Dreams*, p. 33.

[46] See the ninth chapter of Culler's *Pursuit of Signs*.

[47] See Barthes, *Pleasure of the Text*, p. 9: "Is not the most erotic portion of the body *where the garment gapes*?" (emphasis original).

[48] On which see *Lydgate's Temple of Glas*, ed. Schick, p. xx; Bianco, "Black Monk," p. 65; and Symons, *Chaucerian Dream Visions*, p. 87, for the correct identification and translation of line and folio numbers.

Lydgate's poem can therefore seem evasive, but beguilingly so, becoming a vicarious source of frustration, affection, confusion, and enjoyment to the attentive audience.

VERSIFICATION AND STYLE

The poet was among the first to acknowledge that he is not a fine metrist, declaring in the *Troy Book*: "For wel wot I moche þing is wrong, / Falsly metrid, boþe of short and long."[49] Lydgate has often been taken at his word, though it is noteworthy that such professions of inadequacy are commonplace and may themselves imitate Chaucer (e.g., "Though som vers fayle in a sillable" [*The House of Fame*, line 1098]).[50] In fact Lydgate's early admirers thought he equaled Chaucer's brilliance as a versifier, but since the nineteenth century scholars have tended to have a much lower opinion of Lydgate's versification and style while elevating their esteem of Chaucer. Lydgate has indeed become notorious for his metrical irregularity, though without further study of the manuscripts it is difficult to say how much variation is attributable to the poet rather than scribes. *The Temple of Glas* is designed on the pattern of iambic pentameter, but in practice there is considerable variation in stress and syllable count. Several accounts of Lydgate's tendencies have been offered. For example, Schirmer thought that, in general, Lydgate emphasizes accentual rather than syllabic regularity; MacCracken supposed that Lydgate freely mixed four-beat and five-beat lines; Manzalaoui proposed that Lydgate capitalizes on the flexibility inherent in Chaucer's verse.[51] More recently, Duffell has argued that Lydgate's verse design is different from Chaucer's, and so we should not judge one by the standard of the other. Duffell develops the idea that language change in the fifteenth century (especially the loss of the final *–e* resulting in the creation of monosyllabic out of disyllabic words) meant that Lydgate could not have followed Chaucer's rules of versification.[52]

The Temple of Glas is best approached by recognizing that its verse design makes allowances for a great amount of variation in syllable count: i.e., the majority of lines fall in five-stress units, whether or not they are decasyllabic. The challenge of reading Lydgate's verse, then, has always been getting the stress right. Lines that deviate from the iambic rhythm tend themselves to recur regularly enough to have resulted in a critical typology, though one must be cautious about such schemata.[53] The most characteristic variation is known pejoratively as "broken backed," and it is common enough in his works to have been dubbed "Lydgatian." These lines have a caesura or "void position" at the midpoint (e.g., lines 3, 196, 787). As ever, the rhythm of verse is subject in part to the reader's voicing, and there are

---

[49] *Troy Book* 5.3483–84. For another discussion of meter and style, see Schirmer, *John Lydgate*, pp. 70 ff.

[50] On the particular importance of self-deprecation and professions of dullness (or the "humility topos") in fifteenth-century writing, see Lawton, "Dullness and the Fifteenth Century."

[51] Schirmer, *John Lydgate*, p. 73; Lydgate, *Minor Poems*, ed. MacCracken, p. viii; Manzalaoui, "Lydgate and English Prosody," 87–104.

[52] Duffell, "Lydgate's Metrical Inventiveness," pp. 240 ff. Earlier discussed by Schick in *Lydgate's Temple of Glas*, p. lxxiv, but not accepted as a real obstacle or extenuating factor.

[53] A five-type schema is developed by Schick in his edition, *Lydgate's Temple of Glas*, pp. liv–lxiii, but he admits that many lines falling in one category can with different emphasis fall just as well into another.

ways of pronouncing many words that can increase or decrease syllable count, if need be. This may make it sound as though reading Lydgate requires special training or initiation, but the verse can mostly be taken as its own guide; readers must use their ears. Bergen believes that when the verse is given the appropriate delivery, due to the potential for elision, synizesis, syncope, and other ways of realizing unstressed vowels, Lydgate's lines are overwhelmingly regular and thus do not require frequent editorial emendation.[54]

The poem alternates between two styles of verse: rhyming couplets that are reserved for narrative description and are also used in the male lover's soliloquy and seven-line stanzas called rhyme royal (or Chaucerian stanzas) that are used for speeches and lyric set pieces. Near the end of the poem is a ballade consisting of rhyme royal stanzas with a refrain. The combination of verse forms owes perhaps more to French than to English, Chaucerian influence.[55] The personal pleas and prayers in stanza form are full of grace and sophistication, demonstrating "daliaunce" (line 291), or the attractive courtly virtue of verbal dexterity and discretion. Lewis is typical in speaking of the "superiority of stanzaic speeches and dialogues over the poet's own narration in couplets," for most agree that if it were not for the demands of the complex stanzas Lydgate's prolixity would have got the better of him.[56]

Indeed the work eschews what Schirmer refers to as Lydgate's "late style" with its pretentious polysyllables, archaic diction, and general ostentation.[57] However, *The Temple of Glas* does have a few examples of Lydgate's characteristically elastic and sometimes involuted syntax, although readers of modern poetry and fiction should not find such passages very taxing.[58] Pearsall has occasion to speak of the poet's "compulsive accumulation" or "encyclo-paedism," exemplified in the way references pile up seemingly without purpose.[59] For example, in Lydgate's account of the temple mural the painted lovers are catalogued as though for the sake of quantity rather than for sense or sequence, putatively so unlike the way Chaucer does things: e.g., as in Dorigen's lament in The Franklin's Tale. Lydgate has long been criticized for being voluminous and verbose and for going off on tangents — so it has also come as some relief to critics that this poem is so short. Nor does it rely too heavily on narrational description, giving the poet few opportunities to digress or overwork his verse.

Because of the preponderance of speech over narration in *The Temple of Glas*, it may be said to have the dramatic quality of a court masque or mumming. Large tracts of the poem are given over to figures whose action is limited to monologues, interlocutory appeals, and pantomimic gesture. In the elaborate costuming and the careful disposition of characters "on stage" there is something of the austerity of a *tableau vivant*. In the end Lydgate's poetry yields to music making, when the dream comes to a close with a choric ballade sung by the gods in what has to be imagined as a moment of supreme aural and visual spectacle. Lyd-

---

[54] See Lydgate's *Fall of Princes*, ed. Bergen, pp. xxx–xliv.

[55] Bianco, "Black Monk," pp. 65–66, observes that mixed verse forms are not favored or employed at all in those works of Chaucer (i.e., *House of Fame*, *Legend of Good Women*, and *Parliament of Fowls*) that most influenced Lydgate's *Temple of Glas*.

[56] Lewis, *Allegory of Love*, p. 240.

[57] Schirmer, *John Lydgate*, p. 76.

[58] See Couormont, "Studies on Lydgate's Syntax," pp. 134–37; *Lydgate's Temple of Glas*, ed. Schick, p. cxxxiv; and Hardman, "Lydgate's Uneasy Syntax," pp. 12-35.

[59] Pearsall, *John Lydgate* (1970), p. 40.

gate, a writer of several "semi-dramatic" performance pieces (mummings, pageants, pictorial poems, allegorical masques, ceremonial verses), was familiar with the potentialities of drama and probably would have been alive to the theatrical possibilities of this poem.[60]

But the reliance on direct speech, dialogue, and song over physical action has been criticized, for it is a common complaint that *The Temple of Glas* lacks narrative momentum. "There is no action, in fact no movement at all."[61] Actually, it is not strictly true that no story unfolds. The lovers and the dreamer himself move and are moved to take up positions, change perspectives, and experience new sensations. The speeches also indicate, albeit obliquely, that some momentous things are happening: for example, the man says he has just been smitten by the sight of a lady, and later it is implied that some time has passed in which he has been able to prove his fidelity. It is true that not much action is directly reported, but not that no action is represented: the temporal, spatial, and physical coordinates of real events are just abstracted to the level of allegory. Moreover, as I have suggested throughout, perhaps the most important things that happen occur to the reader in the act of interpreting the poem.

HISTORY OF THE TEXT

The popularity of the *The Temple of Glas* is attested by the fact that the poem survives complete in seven manuscripts and several early printed versions; fragments are preserved in other manuscripts and indicate that the poem was something to be plundered and used piecemeal. The bibliography below lists the known texts. A fuller description of the manuscripts and printed editions is given by Schick, pp. xvii–xxx.[62]

On the initiative of the author or scribes, the poem had early evolved into three separate versions, each of which may have had discrete purposes or clientele.[63] The variation between them is chiefly found in the lady's complaint and accoutrements, as well as in the poem's conclusion. Norton-Smith's influential 1958 article on "Lydgate's Changes in the *Temple of Glas*" proposes a particular set of affiliations between the three versions of the poem and concludes that they represent Lydgate's tinkering and progressive improvements (in a first, intermediary, and final draft). Recent scholars have registered doubts about the assumptions that informed Norton-Smith's classification, but his article remains an important point of reference and a useful account of the texts.[64] Part of the problem with trying to date and describe the manuscripts is as much hermeneutic as a result of the lack of historical detail: critical opinions rest on circular arguments about possible occasions and commissions.

---

[60] For introductions to the drama, see Schirmer, *John Lydgate*, pp. 100–08, and Pearsall, *John Lydgate* (1970), pp. 183–88.

[61] Pearsall, *John Lydgate* (1970), p. 109; Spearing, *Medieval Dream-Poetry*, p. 172; Davidoff, *Beginning Well*, p. 138.

[62] See also *John Lydgate: Poems*, ed. Norton-Smith, p. 176; Renoir and Benson, "John Lydgate." p. 2160; Pearsall, *John Lydgate* (1997), p. 79. The fragments are found in the first four folia of British Library MS Sloane 1212, on which see Seaton, *Sir Richard Roos*, p. 376, and Pearsall, *John Lydgate* (1970), p. 18; and in National Library of Scotland Advocates 1.1.6.

[63] Bianco, "New Perspectives," p. 104.

[64] See Boffey, *Fifteenth-Century English Dream Visions*, p. 19; Bianco, "New Perspectives," p. 104.

Mention should also be made of the short *Compleynt* appended to the end of two copies of *The Temple of Glas* (see bibliography).[65] This poem expresses the grief of a man for his absent lady and seems to have been treated by the scribes as a continuation of *The Temple of Glas*. Scholars agree that it is not Lydgate's.

This Middle English Texts Series edition presents the copy of *The Temple of Glas* as preserved in Oxford, Bodleian Library, MS Tanner 346, a manuscript whose description can be found in the introduction to Pamela Robinson's facsimile edition. Tanner is an anthology of love poetry, containing *The Legend of Good Women* among other Chaucerian pieces, and is datable to the second quarter of the fifteenth century. Two previous editors have chosen the same manuscript for their editions. Schick, who edited *The Temple of Glas* for the Early English Text Society, argued that Tanner is the oldest and best of the manuscripts, and Norton-Smith, who produced his edition in 1966, believed this copy of *The Temple of Glas* represents the final and finest draft of the poem. Lerer makes much of the centrality of *The Temple of Glas* within the manuscript as a whole: he argues that the poem is positioned as "the kernel of the collection."[66] But other manuscript versions have their importance. British Library, MS Add. 16165 contains an early version that was copied by John Shirley, who may have known Lydgate. It may represent the first version of the poem, but in any case offers an interesting set of comparisons. In the explanatory notes I provide transcriptions of passages taken from this copy where it deviates from Tanner in its account of the lady's complaint, dress, motto, and garland.

Tanner was chosen as a base-text not because it is aesthetically superior or historically more significant. This edition serves its purpose by making widely available a version of *The Temple of Glas* that has long been out of print. A fine edition of an alternative and possibly earlier version (based on BL Add. 16165) has been published recently.[67]

NOTES ON THE PRESENTATION OF THE TEXT

This edition of *The Temple of Glas* follows the editorial conventions of the Middle English Texts Series in modernizing special Middle English characters (i.e., thorn [þ] and yogh [ȝ]) and in normalizing the letters *i/j* and *u/v*. The scribal ampersand is replaced with *and* (e.g., line 38), and contractions are marked with an apostrophe (e.g., lines 449–50). Words ending in a single long syllabic final *-e* are marked with an accent (e.g., *pité*) to indicate pronunciation. And a final *-e* is added to distinguish the pronoun *thee* from the article *the*. Double consonants at the beginning of a line have been treated as capitals, so, for example, the manuscript reading *fful* is printed *Ful*. Suspension marks and common abbreviations have been silently expanded where they are not otiose. Capitalization and word division are editorial, and the punctuation is modern.

With MS Tanner 346 as the base-text I have found it feasible and desirable to use a conservative policy of emendation. Two manuscripts with which Tanner shares a family resemblance (together forming the so-called "Oxford Group") were consulted when a particular

---

[65] This appended *Compleynt* should not be confused with Lydgate's *A Complaynte of a Lovers Lyfe* (or *The Complaint of the Black Knight*), which also appears in many of the same manuscripts. See Symons, *Chaucerian Dream Visions*, p. 89-90.

[66] Lerer, *Chaucer and His Readers*, p. 68.

[67] Edited by Boffey, *Fifteenth-Century English Dream Visions*, pp. 15–89.

crux, mechanical error, or omission was encountered.[68] Notably, Tanner omits several lines (96, 154, 216, 320) that had to be supplied from the other manuscripts. Emendations were otherwise made where sense blatantly required or there had been misspelling. Final -*e* has been added as required for meter.

MANUSCRIPTS AND EARLY PRINTS

Manuscripts indexed as item 851 in Boffey and Edwards, *A New Index of Middle English Verse*:

- G: Cambridge, University Library, MS Gg. 4. 27, fols. 491r–509v. 1420–25. [Norton-Smith thinks this represents the first version; it is one of two copies that append the *Compleynt* as though it were a continuation of *The Temple of Glas*. For a facsimile, see *Poetical Works of Geoffrey Chaucer*, intro. Parkes and Beadle.]
- S: London, British Library, MS Additional 16165, fols. 206v–241v. 1450. [Norton-Smith thinks this represents the first version of the poem; it is identified as the work of John Shirley and includes the only other copy of the *Compleynt*.]
- F: Oxford, Bodleian Library, MS Fairfax 16, fols. 63r–82v. 1450s. *SC* 3896. [Norton-Smith thinks this represents the intermediate version of the poem, and it belongs to the so-called "Oxford Group" with B and T. For a facsimile see *Bodleian Library MS Fairfax 16*, intro. Norton-Smith.]
- B: Oxford, Bodleian Library, MS Bodley 638, fols. 16v–38r. 1470–80. *SC* 2078. [Norton-Smith thinks this represents the intermediate version of the poem, but it was copied later than either T or F. For a facsimile see *Manuscript Bodley 638: A Facsimile*, intro. Pamela Robinson.]
- T: Oxford, Bodleian Library, MS Tanner 346, fols. 76r–97r. 1440s. *SC* 10173. [Norton-Smith thinks this represents the final version of the poem. For a facsimile see *Manuscript Tanner 346: A Facsimile*, intro. Pamela Robinson.]
- L: Longleat, Warminster, Library of the Marquis of Bath, MS 258, fols. 1r–32r. 1460–70. [Norton-Smith thinks this represents the final version of the poem.]
- SL: London, British Library, MS Sloane 1212, fols. 1, 2, 4. Fifteenth cent. [Fragments of the poem and of the *Compleynt*.]
- P: Cambridge, Magdalene College, MS Pepys 2006, pp. 17–52. 1470–1500. [Norton-Smith thinks this represents the final version of the poem. For a facsimile see *Manuscript Pepys 2006: A Facsimile*, intro. A. S. G. Edwards.]
- BAN: National Library of Scotland Advocates 1.1.6, fol. 220v. (Bannatyne MS.) 1568. [Fragment of the poem starting at line 743.]

Early prints indexed in Pollard and Redgrave, eds., *A Short-Title Catalogue of Books Printed in England, Scotland, and Ireland and of English Books Printed Abroad, 1475–1640*:

- *The temple of glas*. Westminster: William Caxton, 1477. (*STC* 17032)
- *Here begynneth the Temple of glas*. Westminster: Wynkyn de Worde, 1495. (*STC* 17032a)
- *Here begynneth the Temple of glas*. London: Wynkyn de Worde, 1506. (*STC* 17033.7)

---

[68] See *MS Tanner 346*, ed. Robinson, p. xxiv, for the hypothesis that Tanner shares with Fairfax and Bodley a common ancestor in a lost "Oxford" archetype.

- *The temple of glas*. London: Rycharde Pynson, 1503. (*STC* 17033.3)
- *This boke called the Te[m]ple of glasse, is in many places amended, and late diligently imprinted.* London: Thomas Berthelet, 1529. (*STC* 17034; see also *STC* 12955)

	For thought, constreint, and grevous hevines,	*anxiety, distress; severe*
	For pensifhede and for heigh distres,	*melancholy; high (great)*
	To bed I went nou this othir nyght,	*now*
	Whan that Lucina with hir pale light	
5	Was joyned last with Phebus in Aquarie,	*Was last united*
	Amyd Decembre, when of Januarie	*Amid; when concerning*
	Ther be kalendes of the nwe yere,	*expectations*
	And derk Diane, ihorned, nothing clere,	*dark; horned, not at all*
	Had hir bemys undir a mysty cloude.	*Had her beams [concealed]*
10	Within my bed for sore I gan me shroude,	*sorrow; I did cover myself*
	Al desolate for constreint of my wo,	*for the oppression*
	The longe nyght waloing to and fro,	*turning*
	Til atte last, er I gan taken kepe,	*before I began to take notice*
	Me did oppresse a sodein dedeli slepe,	*sudden deathlike*
15	Within the which me thoughte that I was	
	Ravysshid in spirit in a temple of glas	*Taken up*
	(I nyst how, ful fer in wildirnesse)	*knew not; far (distant) [it was]*
	That foundid was, as bi liklynesse,	*established; as it appeared*
	Not opon stele, but on a craggy roche	*steel (iron firmness); rock*
20	Like ise ifrore. And as I did approche	*frozen ice*
	Again the sonne that shone, me thought, so clere	*Against*
	As eny cristal, and ever nere and nere	*nearer*
	As I gan neigh this grisli dredful place,	*did approach*
	I wex astonyed: the light so in my face	*became amazed (dazed)*
25	Bigan to smyte, so persing ever in one	*strike; piercing continuously*
	On evere part, where that I gan gone,	*On every; wherever I went*
	That I ne myght nothing, as I would,	
	Abouten me considre and bihold	
	The wondre hestres, for brightnes of the sonne;	*wondrous surroundings; sun*
30	Til atte last certein skyes donne,	*dark clouds*
	With wind ichaced, have her cours iwent	*By; dispelled; their course turned*
	Tofore the stremes of Titan and iblent,	*Before; obscured [them]*
	So that I myght, within and withoute,	
	Where so I walk, biholden me aboute,	*behold around me*
35	Forto report the fasoun and manere	*To report the appearance*
	Of al this place that was circulere	

In compaswise, round b'entaile wrought.[1]
And whan that I hade long gone and sought,
I fond a wiket and entrid in as fast   *wicket (small gate)*
40   Into the temple, and myn eighen cast   *eyes gazed*
On evere side, now lowe and eft aloft.   *then high*
And right anone as I gan walken soft   *as soon; to walk slowly*
(If I the soth aright reporte shal)   *truth precisely (assuredly)*
I saughe depeynt opon everé wal,   *painted upon every*
45   From est to west, ful many a faire image
Of sondri lovers, lich as thei were of age,   *i.e., come of age*
Isette in ordre aftir thei were trwe,   *Arranged in the degree that*
With lifli colours wondir fressh of hwe.   *lifelike*
And (as me thought) I saughe somme sit and stonde,
50   And some kneling with billis in hir honde,   *petitions (written pleas)*
And some with compleint, woful and pitous,
With doleful chere to putten to Venus,
So as she sate fleting in the se,   *sat floating; sea*
Upon hire wo forto have pité.   *their; pity*
55   And first of al I saugh there of Cartage
Dido the quene, so goodli of visage,   *beautiful of face (demeanor)*
That gan complein hir adventure and caas,   *situation (chance, fate)*
Hou she deceyved was of Eneas,
For al his hestis and his othis sworne,   *Despite; vows; oaths*
60   And said, alas, that ever she was borne,
Whan that she saugh that ded she moste be.
And next I saugh the compleint of Medee,
Hou that she was falsed of Jason.   *deceived by*
And nygh bi Venus saugh I sit Addoun,   *nearby; Adonis*
65   And al the maner hou the bore him slough,   *boar [killed him]*
For whom she wepte and hade pein inoughe.   *pain enough*
There saugh I also, hou Penalopé,
For she so long hir lord ne myghte se,   *Because*
Ful oft wex of colour pale and grene.   *often became (varied)*
70   And aldernext was the fresshe quene,   *next of all; joyous*
I mene Alceste, the noble trwe wyfe,
And for Admete hou she lost hir life,
And for hir trouth, if I shal not lie,
Hou she was turnyd to a daiesie.   *daisy*
75   Ther was also Grisildis innocence,
And al hir mekenes and hir pacience.
There was eke Isaude, and meni anothir mo,
And al the turment and al the cruel wo
That she hade for Tristram al hir live.
80   And hou that Tesbie her herte dide rife   *pierce (split)*

---

[1] *In shape of a sphere, constructed round in form*

	With thilke swerd of him Piramus.	
	And al the maner hou that Theseus	
	The Minatawre slow amyd the hous	*slew; house [of Daedalus (Labyrinth)]*
	That was forwrynkled bi craft of Dedalus,	*twisted (convoluted, coiled)*
85	When that he was in prison shette in Crete.	*shut*
	And hou that Phillis felt of loves hete	*love's heat*
	The grete fire of Demophon, alas,	
	And for his falshed and for his trespas	*falsehood; transgression*
	Upon the walles depeint men myghte se	
90	Hou she was honged upon a filbert tre.	*hanged; filbert (hazel) tree*
	And mani a stori (mo then I rekin can)	*count*
	Were in the tempil. And hou that Paris wan	*won*
	The faire Heleyne, the lusti fresshe quene;	*beautiful; attractive (amorous)*
	And hou Achilles was for Policene	
95	Islain unwarli within Troie toune:	*Slain unexpectedly*
	Al this sawe I walkynge up and doun.	
	Ther sawe I writen eke the hole tale,	
	Hou Philomene into a nyghtyngale	
	Iturned was, and Progne unto a swalow.	
100	And hou the Sabyns in hir maner halowe	*their; honor (celebrate)*
	The fest of Lucresse yit in Rome toune.	*feast day; still*
	There saugh I also the sorou of Palamoun,	
	That he in prison felt, and al the smert,	
	And hou that he thurugh unto his hert	
105	Was hurt unwarli thurugh casting of an eyghe	
	Of faire fressh the yunge Emelie,	
	And al the strife bitwene him and his brothir,	
	And hou that one faught eke with that othir	
	Within the grove, til thei bi Theseus	*wooded area*
110	Acordid were, as Chaucer tellith us.	
	And forthirmore (as I gan bihold),	
	I sawgh hou Phebus with an arow of gold	
	Iwoundid was thurughoute in his side,	*deeply*
	Onli bi envie of the god Cupide;	
115	And hou that Daphne unto a laurer tre	*laurel tree*
	Iturned was when that she dide fle;	
	And hou that Jove gan to chaunge his cope	*cloak (appearance)*
	Oonli for love of the faire Europe,	*Specifically*
	And into a bole, when he did hir sue,	*bull; pursue*
120	List of his godhode his fourme to transmwe;	*Preferred [out] of his divinity*
	And hou that he bi transmutacioun	
	The shap gan take of Amphitrioun	
	For his Almen so passing of beauté;	*outstanding*
	So was he hurt for al his deité	*injured despite; godliness*
125	With loves dart, and myght it not ascape;	*love's arrow*
	There saugh I also hou that Mars was take	*captured*
	Of Vulcanus and with Venus found,	*By*

And with the cheynes invisible bound.
Ther was also al the poesie   *poetry*
130   Of him, Mercurie, and Philologye,
And hou that she for hir sapience   *wisdom*
Iweddit was to god of eloquence,
And hou the Musis lowli did obeie,   *humbly*
High into heven this ladi to convei,   *escort (communicate)*
135   And with hir song hou she was magnified   *exalted*
With Jubiter to bein istellified.   *set among stars (glorified)*
And uppermore depeint men myghte se   *farther up*
Hou with hir ring goodli Canacé
Of everé foule the ledne and the song   *every bird; language*
140   Coud undirstond as she welk hem among;   *walked among them*
And hou hir brothir so oft holpen was   *aided*
In his myschefe bi the stede of bras.   *steed of brass*
And forthermore in the tempil were
Ful mani a thousand of lovers here and there,
145   In sondri wise redi to complein   *various manners*
Unto the goddes of hir wo and pein,   *goddess about their woe*
Hou thei were hindrid, some for envie,
And hou the serpent of fals Jelousie
Ful many a lover hath iput obak,   *impeded*
150   And causeles on hem ilaid a lak.   *without reason; placed blame*
And some ther were that pleyned on absence,
That werin exiled and put oute of presence
Thurugh wikkid tungis and fals suspecioun,
Withoute mercy or remyssyoun.   *release (grant of freedom)*
155   And other eke her servise spent in vain,
Thurugh cruel Daunger and also bi Disdain;   *Resistance*
And some also that loved, soth to sein,
And of her ladi were not lovyd again.   *in return*
And othir eke that for poverté
160   Durst on no wise hir grete adversité   *Dared in no way*
Discure ne open lest thai were refusid;   *Disclose nor expose in case*
And some for wanting also werin accusid,   *lacking [means or qualities]*
And othir eke that loved secreli,
And of her ladi durst aske no merci,   *dared ask*
165   Lest that she would of hem have despite;   *contempt*
And some also that putten ful grete wite   *put great blame*
On double lovers that love thingis nwe,   *Upon deceitful*
Thurgh whos falsnes hindred be the trwe.
And some ther were, as it is ofte found,
170   That for her ladi meny a blodi wounde   *their*
Endurid hath in mani a regioun,
Whiles that an other hath poscessioun   *other [suitor]*
Al of his ladi and berith awai the fruyte
Of his labur and of al his suyte.   *suit*

175	And other eke compleyned on Riches,	
	Hou he with tresour doth his besines	
	To wynnen al againes kynd and ryght,	*against nature (kindness)*
	Wher trw lovers have force noon ne myght.	
	And some ther were as maydens yung of age,	
180	That pleined sore with peping and with rage,	*piping (shrieking)*
	That thei were coupled ageines al nature	*contrary to natural law*
	With croked elde, that may not long endure	*crooked age*
	Forto perfourme the lust of loves plai:	*sexual activity*
	For it ne sit not unto fresshe May	
185	Forto be coupled to oold Januari.	
	Thei ben so divers that thei moste varie,	
	For eld is grucching and malencolious,	*grumbling (irritable); angry*
	Ay ful of ire and suspecious,	*Always; anger*
	And iouth entendeth to joy and lustines,	*inclines toward*
190	To myrth and plai and to al gladnes.	
	Allas that ever that it shulde fal,	
	To soote sugre icoupled be with gal.	*sweet sugar to be; bitterness*
	These yonge folk criden ofte sithe	*frequently*
	And praied Venus hir pouer forto kithe	*power to make known*
195	Upon this myschef and shape remedie.	
	And right anon I herd othir crie	
	With sobbing teris and with ful pitous soune,	*sound*
	Tofore the goddes bi lamentacioun,	*Before the goddess*
	That conseiles in hir tender youthe,	*Who without judgment*
200	And in childhode (as it is oft couthe)	*often known*
	Yrendred were into religioun	*Delivered [they] were*
	Or thei hade yeris of discresioun,	*Before they had [attained]*
	That al her life cannot but complein,	*[So] that*
	In wide copis perfeccion to feine:	*ostentatious robes; pretend*
205	Ful covertli to curen al hir smert	*secretly to cover*
	And shew the contrarie outward of her hert.	*display; outwardly*
	Thus saugh I wepen many a faire maide,	
	That on hir freendis al the wite thei leide.	*guilt they attributed*
	And other next I saugh there in gret rage,	*other [persons]*
210	That thei were maried in her tendir age	*[For the reason] that*
	Withoute fredom of eleccioun,	*freedom to choose*
	Wher love hath seld domynacioun:	*[Which is] where; rarely*
	For love, at laarge and at liberté,	*unrestrained and free*
	Would freli chese and not with such treté.	*choose freely; negotiation*
215	And other saugh I ful oft wepe and wring	*wring [their hands]*
	That they in men founde swych variynge,	*[For the reason] that*
	To love a seisoun while that beauté floureth,	
	And bi disdein so ungoodli loureth	*[he] rudely scowls*
	On hir that whilom he callid his ladi dere,	*formerly*
220	That was to him so plesaunt and entere;	*perfect (beloved)*
	But lust with fairnes is so overgone,	*overcome*

That in her hert trouth abideth none.   *their; remains no more*
And som also I saugh in teris reyne,   *rain*
And pitousli on God and Kynde pleyne,   *Nature*
225   That ever thei would on eny creature
So mych beauté, passing bi mesure,   *beyond measure*
Set on a woman to geve occasioun   *create an opportunity*
A man to love to his confusioun,
And nameli there where he shal have no grace;   *especially*
230   For with a loke forthbi as he doth pace,   *passing look*
Ful ofte falleth, thurugh casting of an yghe,
A man is woundid that he most nedis deye,
That never efter, peraventure, shal hir se.   *as happens by chance*
Whi wil God don so gret a cruelté
235   To eny man or to his creature,
To maken him so mych wo endure,
For hir percaas whom he shal in no wise   *perchance*
Rejoise never, but so forth in jewise   *torment (punishment)*
Ledin his life til that he be grave?   *buried*
240   For he ne durst of hir no merci crave,
And eke, peraventure, though he durst and would
He can not wit where he hir finde shuld.
I saugh there eke (and therof hade I routhe)
That som were hindred for covetise and slouth,   *greed and sloth*
245   And some also for her hastines,
And other eke for hir reklesnes.
But alderlast as I walk and biheld,   *last of all*
Beside Pallas with hir cristal sheld
Tofore the statue of Venus set on height,   *Before*
250   Hou that ther knelid a ladi in my syght
Tofore the goddes, which right as the sonne
Passeth the sterres and doth hir stremes donne,
And Lucifer to voide the nyghtes sorow
In clerenes passeth erli bi the morow;[1]
255   And so as Mai hath the sovereinté
Of evere moneth, of fairnes and beauté;
And as the rose in swetnes and odoure
Surmounteth floures, and bawme of al licour   *Surpasses; balm; liquid*
Haveth the pris; and as the rubie bright   *prize (superiority)*
260   Of al stones in beauté and in sight
(As it is know) hath the regalie: *royalty*
Right so this ladi with hir goodli eighe   *eyes*
And with the stremes of hir loke so bright
Surmounteth al thurugh beauté in my sighte.

---

[1] Lines 251–54: *Before the goddess, who just as the sun / Passes the stars and dulls their rays, / And in order to take away the sorrow of the night, / Surpasses Lucifer in brightness early in the morning*

265	Forto tel hir gret semelines,	*attractiveness*
	Hir womanhed, hir port, and hir fairnes,	*womanliness, her deportment*
	It was a mervaile hou ever that Nature	
	Coude in hir werkis make a creature	
	So aungellike, so goodli on to se,	*look*
270	So femynyn or passing of beauté,	
	Whos sonnyssh here, brighter than gold were	*luminous hair; wire*
	Lich Phebus bemys shynyng in his spere;	*sphere*
	The goodlihed eke of hir fresshli face,	*excellence; radiant*
	So replenysshid of beauté and of grace,	
275	So wel ennuyd bi Nature and depeint	*colored; painted*
	That rose and lileis togedir were so meint,	*combined*
	So egalli bi good proporcioun	*equally*
	That (as me thought) in myn inspeccioun	
	I gan mervaile hou God or werk of Kynd	
280	Mighten of beauté such a tresour find,	
	To geven hir so passing excellence.	
	For, in goode faith, thurugh hir heigh presence	
	The tempil was enlumynd enviroun.	*illuminated all around*
	And forto speke of condicioun	
285	She was the best that myghte ben on lyve:	*alive*
	For ther was noon that with hir myghte strive,	*rival*
	To speke of bounté or of gentilles,	*generosity; nobility*
	Of womanhed or of lowlynes,	
	Of curtesie or of goodlihed,	
290	Of spech, of chere, or of semlyhed,	*cheer; seemliness*
	Of port benygne and of daliaunce	*gracious; conversation*
	The beste taught, and therto of plesaunce	
	She was the wel, and eke of onesté	*wellspring (source)*
	An exemplarie, and mirrour eke was she	
295	Of secrenes, of trouth, of faythfulnes,	*discretion*
	And to al other ladi and maistres,	*teachers*
	To sue vertu, whoso list to lere.	*With regard to; learn*
	And so this ladi benigne and humble of chere,	
	Kneling I saugh, al clad in grene and white,	
300	Tofore Venus, goddes of al delite,	
	Embrouded al with stones and perre	*Ornamented; jewels*
	So richeli that joi it was to se,	
	With sondri rolles on hir garnement	*scrolls*
	Forto expoune the trouth of hir entent,	*expound*
305	And shew fulli that for hir humbilles,	
	And for hir vertu and hir stabilnes,	
	That she was rote of al womanli pleasaunce.	*root*
	Therfore hir woord withoute variaunce	*motto*
	Enbrouded was, as men myghte se,	*Embroidered*
310	*De Mieulx en Mieulx*, with stones and perre.	*From Better to Better*
	This to sein that she, this benigne,	*gracious [woman]*

From bettir to bettir hir herte doth resigne   *yield*
And al hir wil to Venus the goddes,
Whan that hir list hir harmes to redresse.
315   For, as me thought, sumwhat bi hir chere,   *countenance*
Forto compleyne she hade gret desire:
For in hir hond she held a litel bil   *bill (written plea)*
Forto declare the somme of al hir wil   *sum*
And to the goddes hir quarel forto shewe,   *complaint*
320   Th'effect of which was this in wordys fewe:

"O ladi Venus, modir of Cupide,
That al this world hast in governaunce,
And hertes high that hauteyn ben of pride   *are arrogant out of pride*
Enclynyst mekeli to thin obeissaunce,   *Incline [proud hearts]*
325   Causer of joie, releser of penaunce,
And with thi stremes canst everithing discerne
Thurugh hevenli fire of love that is eterne;

"O blisful sterre, persant and ful of light,   *penetrating*
Of bemys gladsome, devoider of derknes,   *dispeller*
330   Cheif recounford after the blak nyght,   *comfort (consolation)*
To voide woful oute of her hevynes,   *woeful [ones]*
Take nou goode hede, ladi and goddesse,
So that my bil your grace may atteyne,
Redresse to finde of that I me compleyne.

335   "For I am bounde to thing that I nold,   *don't want*
Freli to chese there lak I liberté.   *where*
And so I want of that myn herte would —   *lack; desires*
The bodi knyt, althoughe my thought be fre —   *tied*
So that I most of necessité   *must*
340   Myn hertis lust outward contrarie;   *outwardly contradict*
Thogh we be on, the dede most varie.   *one (united); deed*

"Mi worship sauf, I faile eleccioun;   *honor preserved*
Again al right, bothe of God and Kynd,   *Against*
There to be knit undir subjeccion,
345   Fro whens ferre ar both witte and mynde.   *From whence far*
Mi thought gothe forthe, my bodi is behind,
For I am here and yonde my remembraunce:
Atwixen two so hang I in balaunce.

"Devoide of joie, of wo I have plenté.
350   What I desire, that mai I not possede,   *obtain*
For that I nold is redi aye to me,   *would not is available ever*
And that I love forto swe I drede: *pursue*
To my desire contrarie is my mede.   *reward*

355 And thus I stond departid even on tweyn,   *divided exactly in two [parts]*
Of wille and dede ilaced in a chaine.

"For thoughe I brenne with fervence and with hete,
Within myn hert I mot complein of cold;
And thurugh myn axcesse thoghe I sweltre and swete,   *lovesickness; burn and sweat*
Me to complein, God wot, I am not boold
360 Unto no wight; nor a woord unfold   *no one*
Of al my peyne — allas the harde stond —   *difficult position*
That hatter brenne that closid is my wounde.   *hotter burn; covered*

"For he that hath myn herte feithfulli
And hole my luf in al honesti   *completely [possesses]*
365 Withoute chaunge, albeit secreli,
I have no space with him forto be.
O ladi Venus, consider nou and se
Unto the effecte and compleint of my bil,
Sith life and deth I put al in thi wil."   *Inasmuch as (Since)*

370 And tho me thought the goddes did enclyne   *And then*
Mekeli hir hede, and softli gan expresse
That in short tyme hir turment shulde fyne,   *cease*
And hou of him for whom al hir distresse
Contynued had and al hir hevynes,
375 She would have joy, and of hir purgatorie   *from (out of)*
Be holpen sone and so forth lyve in glorie.   *assisted soon*

And seid: "Doughter, for the sadde trouthe,   *sober devotion*
The feithful menyng and the innocence   *purpose*
That planted bene withouten eny slouthe
380 In your persone, devoide of al defence,   *stubborn resistance*
So have atteyned to oure audience
That thurugh oure grace ye shul be wel relevyd,
I you bihote of al that hath you greved.   *promise*

"And for that ye ever of oon entent,
385 Withoute chaunge of mutabilité
Have in your peynes ben so pacient
To take louli youre adversité,   *humbly (lowly)*
And that so long thurugh the cruelté
Of old Saturne, my fadur, unfortuned: *been visited by misfortune*
390 Your wo shal nou no lenger be contuned.   *continued*

"And thinkith this: within a litel while
It shal asswage and overpassen sone.
For men bi laiser passen meny a myle;   *at length of time (given time)*
And oft also aftir a dropping mone,   *misty (waning) moon*

395   The weddir clereth, and whan the storme is done,
        The sonne shineth in his spere bright;   *sphere*
        And joy awakith whan wo is put to flight.

        "Remembreth eke hou never yit no wight
        Ne came to wirship withoute some debate,
400   And folk also rejosshe more of light
        That thei with derknes were waped and amate.   *stunned and overcome*
        Non manis chaunce is alwai fortunate,
        Ne no wight preiseith of sugre the swetnes
        But thei afore have tasted bitternes.

405   "Grisilde was assaied atte ful,   *tested*
        That turned aftir to hir encrese of joye;
        Penalope gan eke for sorowis dul,   *[to grow] dull*
        For that her lord abode so long at Troie;
        Also the turment there coude no man akoye   *soothe*
410   Of Dorigene, flour of al Britayne: *Brittany*
        Thus ever joy is ende and fine of paine.

        "And trusteth thus, for conclusioun,
        The end of sorow is joi ivoide of drede.
        For holi saintis thurugh her passioun,
415   Have heven iwonne for her soverain mede;   *heaven; supreme reward*
        And plenti gladli foloith after nede.
        And so, my doughter, after your grevauns
        I you bihote ye shul have ful plesaunce.   *promise*

        "For ever of Love the maner and the guyse   *custom*
420   Is forto hurt his servant and to wounde;
        And when that he hath taughte hem his emprise,   *lore (purpose or power)*
        He can in joi make hem to abounde.
        And sith that ye have in my lase be bound   *cord (snare)*
        Withoute grucching or rebellion,
425   Ye most of right have consolacioun.   *must*

        "This is to sein — douteth never a dele —   *not at all*
        That ye shal have ful possession
        Of him that ye cherissh nou so wel
        In honest maner withoute offencioun,   *sin (stumbling)*
430   Bicause I cnowe your entencion
        Is truli set, in parti and in al,
        To love him best and most in special.

        "For he that ye have chosen yow to serve
        Shal be to yow such as ye desire
435   Withoute chaunge, fulli, til he sterve.   *die*

So with my brond I have him set afire,   *torch*
And with my grace I shal him so enspire
That he in hert shal be ryght at your will,
Whethir ye list to save him or to spill.   *desire; kill*

440   "For unto yow his hert I shal so lowe,
       Withoute spot of eny doubelnes,
       That he ne shal escape fro the bowe —
       Though that him list thurugh unstidfastnes —
       I mene of Cupide that shal him so distres
445   Unto your hond, with the arow of gold,
       That he ne shal escapen though he would.

       "And sithe ye list of pité and of grace
       In vertu oonli his youthe to cherice,   *In virtue above all*
       I shal b'aspectes of my benygne face,   *by the influence*
450   Make him t'eschwe evere synne and vice   *shun every*
       So that he shal have no maner spice   *taste*
       In his corage to love thingis nwe:
       He shal to you so plain be found and trwe."

       And whan this goodli faire, fressh of hwe,   *fair [creature]*
455   Humble and benygne, of trouth crop and rote,   *flower and root*
       Conceyved had hou Venus gan to rwe,   *have pity*
       On hir praier plainli to do bote,   *cause relief*
       To chaunge hir bitter atones into soote,   *instantly into sweet*
       She fel on kneis of heigh devocion,
460   And in this wise bigan hir orisoun: *prayer (oration)*

       "Heighest of high, quene and emperice,
       Goddes of love, of goode yit the best,
       That thurugh your beauté, withouten eny vice,
       Whilom conquered the appel at the fest   *Once; apple at the feast*
465   That Jubiter thurugh his hygh request
       To al the goddesse above celestial
       Made in his paleis most imperial: *palace*

       "To you my ladi, upholder of my life,
       Mekeli I thanke, so as I mai suffice,
470   That ye list nou with hert ententif,   *will; attentive heart*
       So graciousli for me to devyse,
       That while I live, with humble sacrifise,
       Upon your auters, your fest yere bi yere,   *altars; feast year by year*
       I shal encense casten in the fire.   *incense cast*

475   "For of youre grace I am ful reconsiled
       From evere trouble unto joy and ease,

That sorois al from me ben exiled,
Sith ye, my ladi, list nou to appese   *appease*
Mi peynes old and fulli my disease
480   Unto gladnes so sodeinli to turne
Havyng no cause from hennes forth to mourne.   *hence*

"For sithin ye so mekeli list to daunte   *since; compel*
To my servyce him that loveth me best,
And of your bounté so graciousli to graunte
485   That he ne shal varie, thoughe him list,
Wherof myn hert is fulli brought to rest:
For nou and ever, o ladi myn benygne,
That hert and wil to yow hole I resigne.   *completely*

"Thanking yow with al my ful hert
490   That of youre grace and visitacioun
So humbeli list him to convert
Fulli to bene at my subjeccioun
Withoute chaunge or transmutacioun
Unto his lust — laude and reverence   *acclaim*
495   Be to youre name and your excellence!

"This al and some and chefe of my request
And hool substaunce of myn hole entent,
Yow thankyng ever of your graunt and hest,   *grant and vow*
Both nou and ever, that ye me grace have sent
500   To conquere him that never shal repent
Me forto serve and humbli to please,
As final tresur to myn hertis ease."

And than anon Venus cast adoune
Into hir lap braunchis white and grene
505   Of hawethorn that wenten enviroun   *all around*
Aboute hir hed, that joi it was to sene,
And bade hir kepe hem honestli and clene:
Which shul not fade ne nevir wexin old
If she hir bidding kepe, as she hath told: *promises*

510   "And as these bowghis be both faire and swete,
Folowith th'effect that thei do specifie:
This is to sein, both in cold and hete,
Beth of oon hert and of o fantasie   *vision (hope)*
As ar these leves the which mai not die   *leaves*
515   Thurugh no dures of stormes that be kene,   *force; are severe*
No more in winter then in somer grene.

	"Right so b'ensaumple for wele or for wo,	*by the example; weal*
	For joy, turment, or for adversité,	
	Wherso that fortune favour or be foo,	*Whether; foe*
520	For povert, riches, or prosperité,	
	That ye youre hert kepe in oo degré	*maintain in one position*
	To love him best, for nothing that ye feine,	
	Whom I have bound so lowe undir youre cheine."	*chain*

	And with that worde the goddes shoke hir hede	
525	And was in peas and spake as tho no more.	*spoke at that time*
	And therwithal, ful femynyne of drede,	*thereupon; womanlike*
	Me thoughte this ladi sighen gan ful sore	*began to sigh deeply*
	And saide again: "Ladi that maist restore	
	Hertes in joy from her adversité,	
530	To do youre will *de mieulx en mieulx magré*."	*(see note)*

EXPLICIT PRIMA PARS   *Here ends the first part*

ICY COMMENCE LE SECUND PARTI DE LA SONGE   *Here begins the second part of the poem*

	Thus ever sleping and dremyng as I lay	
	Within the tempil me thoughte that I sey	*saw*
	Gret pres of folk with murmur wondirful,	*crowd*
	To bronte and showe (the tempil was so ful),	*rush and shove*
535	Everich ful bisé in his owne cause	*Each full of activity*
	That I ne may shortli in a clause	
	Descriven al the rithes and the gise;	*rites and the behavior*
	And eke I want kunnyng to devyse	*lack intelligence*
	Hou som ther were with blood, encense, and mylk,	
540	And som with floures sote and soft as silk,	*flowers sweet*
	And som with sparouis and dovues faire and white,	*sparrows; doves*
	That forto offerin gan hem to delite	
	Unto the goddes with sigh and with praier	
	Hem to relese of that thai most desire.	
545	That for the prese, shortli to conclude,	*That because of the crowd*
	I went my wai for the multitude	*on account of*
	Me to refressh oute of the prese allone.	
	And be myself (me thought) as I gan gone	*by myself; went (began to go)*
	Within the estres and gan awhile tarie,	*precincts (building); loiter*
550	I saugh a man that welke al solitarie,	*walked*
	That as me semed for hevines and dole	*dolefulness*
	Him to complein, that he walk so sole,	*alone*
	Withoute espiing of eni othir wight.	*Escaping notice*
	And if I shal descryven him aright,	
555	Nere that he hade ben in hevynes,	*Were it not*
	Me thought he was, to speke of semelynes,	

Of shappe, of fourme, and also of stature,
The most passing that evir yit Nature   *surpassing [creature]*
Made in hir werkis, and like to ben a man;   *most likely (accordingly)*
560   And therwithal, as I reherse can,
Of face and chere the most gracious
To be biloved, happi and ewrous.   *prosperous*
But as it semed outward in his chere   *outwardly*
That he compleyned for lak of his desire:
565   For by himself as he walk up and doune
I herd him make a lamentacioun,
And seid: "Allas, what thing mai this be?
That nou am bound that whilom was so fre   *once*
And went at laarge at myn eleccioun,
570   Nou am I caught under subjeccioun
Forto bicome a verre homagere   *true servant*
To god o' love — where that, er I come here,   *whereas, before I came*
Felt in myn hert right nought of loves peine.
But nou of nwe within his fire cheyne   *for the first time; fiery*
575   I am embraced, so that I mai not strive
To love and serve whiles that I am on lyve
The goodli fressh in the tempil yonder   *over there*
I saugh right nou, that I hade wonder   *[Whom] I saw*
Hou ever God, forto reken all,   *all things considered*
580   Myght make a thing so celestial,
So aungellike on erthe to appere.
For with the stremes of hir eyen clere
I am iwoundid even to the hert
That fro the deth, I trow, I mai not stert.   *leap [out of the way]*
585   And most I mervaile that so sodenli
I was iyolde to bene at hir merci,   *handed over*
Wherso him list, to do me lyve or deie.   *cause me to*
Withoute more I most hir lust obeie   *will (desire)*
And take mekeli my sodein aventur.
590   For sith my life, my deth, and eke my cure
Is in hir hond, it woulde not availe
To gruch agein: for of this bataile   *grumble against*
The palme is hires and pleinli the victorie.
If I rebelled, honour non ne glorie
595   I myghte not in no wise acheve.
Sith I am yold hou shuld I than preve   *made to yield; try*
To gif a werre — I wot it wil not be —   *put up a fight*
Though I be loos, at laarge I mai not fle.   *loose (unshackled); fly*
O god of love, hou sharp is nou thin arowe;
600   Hou maist thou nou so cruelli and narowe
Withoute cause hurte me and wound,
And take non hede my soris forto sound!   *heed; sorrows to measure*
But lich a brid that fleith at hir desire

	Til sodeinli within the pantire	*bird trap*
605	She is icaught, though she were late at laarge,	
	A nwe tempest forcasteth now my baarge,	*casts forth (tosses)*
	Now up, now doune, with wind it is so blowe,	
	So am I possid and almost overthrowe,	*thrust*
	Fordrive in dirknes with many a sondri wawe.	*wave*
610	Alas, when shal this tempest overdrawe	*pass*
	To clere the skies of myn adversité?	
	The lode-ster, when I may not se,	*lodestar*
	It is so hid with cloudes that ben blake.	
	Alas, when wil this turment overshake?	*pass away*
615	I can not wit, for who is hurt of nwe	
	And bledith inward til he wex pale of hwe	
	And hath his wound unwarli fressh and grene,	*suddenly*
	He is not kouthe unto the harmes kene	*acquainted with*
	Of myghti Cupide that can so hertis daunte,	
620	That no man may in your werre him vaunte	*boast*
	To gete a pris, but oonli bi mekenes.	*Win the prize, except through*
	For there ne vaileth strif ne sturdines,	*avails (helps)*
	So mai I sain, that with a loke am yold	
	And have no power to stryve thoughe I would.	
625	Thus stand I even bitwix life and deth	
	To love and serve while that I have breth,	
	In such a place where I dar not pleyn,	
	Lich him that is in turment and in pein,	
	And knoweth not to whom forto discure.	*divulge (i.e., disclose his secret pain)*
630	For there that I have hoolly set my cure,	
	I dar not wele, for drede and for daunger	*not profitably (fully)*
	And for unknowe, tellen hou the fire	*ignorance*
	Of Lovis brond is kindled in my brest.	*torch*
	Thus am I murdrid and slain at the lest	*at all events*
635	So preveli within myn owne thought.	*So inwardly (undetected)*
	O ladi Venus, whom that I have sought,	
	So wisse me now what me is best to do	*guide*
	That am distraught within myselfen so	
	That I ne wot what way forto turne,	*know*
640	Sauf be myself solein forto mourne	*Left alone; solitary*
	Hanging in balaunce bitwix Hope and Drede	
	Withoute comfort, remedie, or rede.	*advice*
	For Hope biddith pursue and assay;	
	And Drede againward answerith and saith nai.	*in opposition*
645	And now with Hope I am iset on loft,	*on high*
	But Drede and Daunger, hard and nothing softe,	
	Have overthrowe my trust and put adoune.	
	Nou at my laarge, nou feterid in prisone,	
	Nou in turment, nou in soverein glorie,	
650	Nou in paradise and nou in purgatorie,	

As man dispeired in a double werre: *in despair for indecision*
Born up with Hope and than anon Daunger
Me drawith abak and seith it shal not be.
For whereas I, of myn adversité,   *[out] of*
655   Am hold somwhile merci to requere,   *charged sometimes; to ask*
Than cometh Dispeire and ginneth me to lere   *begins to teach me*
A nwe lessoun, to hope full contrarie.
Thei be so divers thei would do me varie.   *contrary; vacillate*
And thus I stond dismaied in a traunce,
660   For whan that Hope were likli me t'avaunce,
For drede I tremble and dar a woord not speke.
And if it so be that I not oute breke
To tel the harmes that greven me so sore,
But in myschef encrese hem more and more   *in adversity*
665   And to be slain fulli me delite,
Then of my deth she is nothing to wite;   *none the wiser*
For but if she my constreint pleinli knwe,   *unless*
Hou shuld she ever opon my paynis rwe?   *upon my pains have pity*
Thus ofte tyme with Hope I am imevid   *moved*
670   To tel hir al of that I am so greved,
And to ben hardi on me forto take   *bold*
To axe merci — but Drede than doth awake
And thorugh wanhope answerith me again,   *despair*
That bettir were, then she have disdeyne,   *better [it] were, than*
675   To deie at onys, unknow of eny wight.
And therewithal bitt Hope anon ryght   *bids*
Me to bihold to prayen hir of grace,
For sith al vertues be portreid in hir face
It were not sitting that merci were bihind.   *appropriate*
680   And right anone within myself I finde
A nwe ple brought on me with Drede,   *put to me by*
That me so maseth that I se no spede,   *bewilders; success*
Bicause he seith — that stoneith al my bloode —   *numbs my body*
I am so symple and she is so goode.
685   Thus Hope and Drede in me wil not ceasse
To plete and stryve myn harmes to encrese.   *plead [a case] (debate)*
But at the hardest yit or I be dede,   *at the least still before*
Of my distresse sith I can no rede,   *since I know no remedy*
But stonde doumb, stil as eni stone,   *still as any*
690   Tofore the goddes I wil me hast anone   *hurry now*
And complein withoute more sermon.
Though deth be fin and ful conclusioun   *final*
Of my request, yit I will assai."
And right anon me thoughte that I say
695   This woful man (as I have memorie)
Ful lowli entre into an oratorie,   *chapel*
And knelid doun in ful humble wise

Tofore the goddes, and gan anon devyse
His pitous quarel with a doleful chere
700 Saying right thus, anone as ye shul here:

"Redresse of sorow, O Citheria,   *[Provide] relief*
That with the stremes of thi plesaunt hete   *heat*
Gladest the contre of al Cirrea   *country*
Where thou hast chosen thi paleis and thi sete,   *seat (residence)*
705 Whos bright bemes ben wasshen and oft wete
In the river of Elicon the wel:
Have nou pité of that I shal here tell.   *that [which]*

"And not disdeyneth of your benignité,
Mi mortal wo, O ladi myn, goddes
710 Of grace and bounté and merciful pité,
Benigneli to helpen and to redresse.
And though so be I can not wele expresse   *notwithstanding; fully*
The grevous harmes that I fele in myn hert,
Haveth nevertheles merci of my smert.

715 "This is to seyn: O clere hevens light
That next the sonne cercled have your spere,   *rounded (set like a circle); sphere*
Sith ye me hurten with your dredful myght
Bi influence of your bemys clere,
And that I bie your servise nou so dere,   *purchase*
720 As ye me brought into this maledie,
Beth gracious and shapeth remedie.

"For in yow hoolli lith help of al this case
And knowe best my sorow and al my peyne:
For drede of deth hou I ne der, allas,
725 To axen merci ones ne me compleyne.
Nou with youre fire hire herte so restreyne —
Withoute more, or I deie at the lest —
That she mai wete what is my requeste: *know*

"Hou I nothing in al this world desire
730 But forto serve fulli to myn ende
That goodli fressh, so womanli of chere,   *young [creature]*
Withoute chaunge, while I have life and mynde;
And that ye wil me such grace send
Of my servyse, that she not disdeyne,
735 Sithen hir to serve I may me not restreyne;

"And sith that Hope hathe geve me hardines
To love hire best and never to repent,
Whiles that I lyve with al my bisenes   *diligence*

To drede and serve, though Daunger never assent.
740   And hereopon ye knowen myn entent,   *vowed*
Hou I have woid fulli in my mynde
To ben hir man though I no merci finde.

"For in myn hert enprentid is so sore
Hir shap, hir fourme, and al hir semelines,
745   Hir port, hir chere, hir goodnes more and more,
Hir womanhede and eke hir gentilnes,
Hir trouth, hir faith and hir kyndenes,
With al vertues iche set in his degré: *each*
There is no lak, save onli of pité.

750   "Hir sad demening, of wil not variable,   *grave (composed)*
Of looke benygne and roote of al plesaunce,
And exemplaire to al that wil be stable,
Discrete, prudent, of wisdom suffisaunce,
Mirrour of wit, ground of governaunce,
755   A world of beauté compassid in hir face,   *contained*
Whose persant loke doth thurugh myn herte race;   *sharp*

"And over this secré and wondre trwe,   *moreover*
A welle of fredome and right bounteuous,
And ever encresing in vertue nwe and nwe,
760   Of spech goodli and wonder gracious,
Devoide of pride, to pore not dispitous;   *the poor not contemptuous*
And if that I shortli shal not feyne,
Save opon merci I nothing can compleyne.

"What wonder than though I be with drede
765   Inli supprised forto axen grace   *overpowered*
Of hir that is a quene of womanhed?
For wele I wot in so heigh a place   *assuredly I know*
It wil not ben; therfor I overpace   *skip over*
And take louli what wo that I endure,   *humbly*
770   Til she of pité me take unto hir cure.   *[out] of; into her keeping*

"But oone avowe pleinli here I make:
That whethir so be she do me lyve or deye,
I wil not grucch but humbeli it take,
And thanke God and wilfulli obey.
775   For be my trouth myn hert shal not reneye,   *relinquish*
For life ne deth, merci nor daunger,
Of wil and thought to ben at hir desire;

"To bene as trwe as ever was Antonyus
To Cleopatre while him lasted brethe;

780   Or unto Tesbé yunge Piramus
       That was feithful found til hem departid dethe;   *until death parted them*
       Right so shal I, til Antropos me sleithe,
       For wele or wo hir faithful man be found,
       Unto my last, lich as myn hert is bounde;

785   "To love as wel as did Achilles
       Unto his last the faire Polixene;
       Or as the gret, famous Hercules
       For Dianyre that felt the shottes kene;   *sharp/bitter darts*
       Right so shal I, y sei right as I mene,
790   Whiles that I lyve, hir bothe drede and serve,
       For lak of merci though she do me sterve.   *destroy*

       "Nou ladi Venus, to whom nothing unknowe
       Is in the world, ihid ne not mai be —   *naught*
       For there nys thing nethir heigh ne lowe   *is nothing*
795   Mai be concelid from your priveté —   *hidden counsel (knowledge)*
       Fro whom my menyng is not nou secré,
       But witen fulli that myn entent is trwe
       And lich my trowth, nou on my peyne rwe.   *have compassion*

       "For more of grace than presumpcioun
800   I axe merci, and not of dueté,   *duty (what is owed)*
       Of louli humblesse, withoute offensioun,
       That ye enclyne, of your benygnyté,
       Your audience to myn humylité
       To graunte me that to you clepe and calle   *hail and call*
805   Somdai relese yit of my paynes alle.

       "And sith ye have the guerdon and the mede   *since; punishment; reward*
       Of al lovers pleinli in your hond,
       Nou of your grace and pité taketh hede
       Of my distresse, that am undir your bond
810   So louli bound — as ye wele undirstond.   *obediently; thoroughly*
       Nou in that place where I toke first my wound
       Of pité sufferith my helth mai be found.   *permit [that]*

       "That lich as she me hurte with a sighte
       Right so with helpe let hir me sustene,
815   And as the stremes of hir eyghen bright
       Whilom myn hert with woundis sharp and kene
       Thurugh perced have — and yit bene fressh and grene —
       So as she me hurt, nou let hir me socoure,   *bring remedy*
       Or ellis certein I mai not long endure.

820   "For lak of spech I can sey nou no more:
        I have mater but I can not plein.
        Mi wit is dulle to telle al my sore.
        A mouth I have and yit for al my peyne,
        For want of woordis I may not nou atteyne
825   To tell half that doth myn herte greve,
        Merci abiding, til she me list releve.   *awaiting; desires to relieve me*

        "But this th'effecte of my mater finalle:
        With deth or merci, reles forto finde.   *release*
        For hert, bodi, thought, life, lust, and alle,
830   With al my reson and alle my ful mynde,
        And five wittes, of oon assent I bind
        To hir service withouten eny strife,
        And make hir princesse of my deth or life.

        "And you I prai of routh and eke pité,
835   O goodli planet, O ladi Venus bright,
        That ye youre sone of his deité —   *son*
        Cupid I mene — that with his dredful myght,
        And with his brond, that is so clere of lighte,
        Hir herte so to fire and to mark,   *aim at (strike)*
840   As ye me whilom brente with a spark:

        "That evenlich and with the same fire,
        She mai be het, as I nou brenne and melt,   *inflamed*
        So that hir hert be flaumed bi desire
        That she mai knowe bi fervence hou I swelt.   *swelter*
845   For of pité pleinli if she felt
        The selfe hete that doth myn hert enbrace,
        I hope of routhe she would do me grace."

        And therwithal Venus (as me thought)
        Toward this man ful benygneli
850   Gan cast hir eyghe, liche as though she rought   *was concerned*
        Of his disease, and seid ful goodeli:
        "Sith it is so that thou so humbelie
        Withoute grucchyng oure hestis list obey,
        Toward thin help I wil anon purvey.   *make provision*

855   "And eke my sone Cupide that is so blind,
        He shal ben helping, fulli to perfourme
        Your hole desire, that nothing behind
        Ne shal be left: so we shal refourme   *remedy*
        The pitous compleint that makith thee to mourne,
860   That she for whom thou soroist most in hert
        Shal thurugh hir merci relese al thi smert   *alleviate*

"Whan she seth tyme thurugh oure purveaunce.   *providence*
Be not to hasti, but suffre alway wele.   *well (faithfully)*
For in abidyng thurugh lowli obeissaunce
865   Lithe ful redresse of al that ye nou fele,
And she shal be as trw as eny stele
To yowe allone, thurugh oure myght and grace,
Yif ye lust mekeli abide a litel space.   *patiently wait awhile*

"But undirstondeth that al hir cherisshing
870   Shal ben groundid opon honesté,
That no wight shal thurugh evil compassing,   *plan*
Demen amys of hir in no degré.
For neither merci, routhe, ne pité
She shal not have, ne take of thee non hede
875   Ferther then longith unto hir womanhede.

"Bethe not astoneid of no wilfulnes,   *(i.e., do not be willful)*
Ne nought dispeired of this dilacioun;   *delay*
Lete reson bridel lust bi buxumnes,   *humility (obedience)*
Withoute grucching or rebellioun,
880   For joy shal folou al this passioun.
For who can suffre turment and endure
Ne mai not faile that folou shal his cure.

"For toforn all she shal thee loven best: *above all*
So shal I here withoute offencioun
885   Bi influence enspiren in hir brest,
In honest wise with ful entencioun,
Forto enclyne bi clene affeccioun
Hir hert fulli on thee to have routhe,
Bicause I know that thou menyst trouthe.

890   "Go nou to hir, where as she stant aside,
With humble chere and put thee in hir grace,
And al biforne late Hope be thi guide,   *in front let*
And thoughe that Drede woulde with thee pace,   *step [alongside]*
It sitteth wel; but loke that thou arace   *erase (pluck out)*
895   Out of thin hert wanhope and dispaire,   *hopelessness*
To hir presence er thou have repaire.   *gone to*

"And Merci first shal thi waie make,
And Honest Menyng aforn do thi message   *beforehand*
To make Merci in hir hert awake;
900   And Secrenes, to further thi viage,   *journey*
With Humble Port to hir that is so sage,
Shul menes ben — and I myself also   *intermediaries*
Shal thee fortune er thi tale be do.   *Give you success before your complaint*

        "Go forthe anon and be right of goode chere,

905   For specheles nothing maist thou spede;

        Be goode of trust and be nothing in were,   *doubt*

        Sith I myself shal helpen in this nede;   *crisis*

        For at the lest of hir goodlihed

        She shal to thee hir audience enclyne,   *listen to you*

910   And louli thee here til thou thi tale fyne.   *hear*

        "Fore wele thou wost, yif I shal not feine,   *know*

        Withoute spech thou maist no merci have:

        For who that wil of his prevé peine   *private (personal)*

        Fulli be cured, his life to help and save,

915   He most mekeli oute of his hurtis grave

        Discure his wound and shew it to his lech,   *physician*

        Or ellis deie for defaute of spech.   *lack*

        "For he that is in myschef rekeles   *misfortune negligent*

        To sechen help, I hold him but a wrecch.

920   And she ne mai thin herte bring in peas

        But if thi compleint to hir herte strecch.   *Unless; extend*

        Wouldist thou be curid and wilte no salve fecch?

        It wil not be: for no wighte may atteyne

        To come to blis if he lust lyve in peyne.

925   "Therfore at ones go in humble wise

        Tofore thi ladi and louli knele adoun,

        And in al trouth thi woordis so devyse

        That she on thee have compassioun:

        For she that is of so heigh renoun

930   In al vertues as quene and soverain,

        Of womanhed shal rwe opon thi pein."

        And whan the goddes this lesson hade him told,

        Aboute me so as I gan bihold,

        Right for-astoneid I stode in a traunce,   *extremely stunned*

935   To sein the maner and the countenaunce

        And al the chere of this woful man,

        That was of hwe deedli pale and wan,

        With drede supprised in his owne thought,   *overwhelmed*

        Making a chere as that he roughte nought   *cared not*

940   Of life ne deth, ne what so him bitide.   *happened*

        So mych fere he hade on everé side,

        To put him forthe forto tel his peyne

        Unto his ladi, other to compleyne   *or*

        What wo he felt, turment or disease,

945   What dedli sorou his herte dide sease —   *seize*

        For routhe of which his wo as I endite,   *compose*

Mi penne I fele quaken as I write.
Of him I had so great compassioun,
Forto reherse his weymentacioun,   *lament*
950   That wel unnethe though with my self I strive,   *with great difficulty*
I want connyng his peynes to discryve.   *lack skill*
Allas, to whom shal I for helpe cal?
Not to the Musis, for cause that thei ar al   *because*
Help of right in joi and not in wo,   *Assistants rightfully*
955   And in maters that thei delite also,
Wherfore thei nyl directe as nou my stile,   *will not; writing style (stylus)*
Nor me enspiren — allas, the harde while.   *difficult time*
I can no ferther but to Thesiphone   *can [go]*
And to hir sustren forto helpe me,
960   That bene goddesses of turment and of peyne.
Nou lete youre teris into myn inke reyne,   *ink rain*
With woful woordis my pauper forto blot,   *paper*
This woful mater to peinte not, but spotte: *write not, but smudge*
To tell the maner of this dredful man,   *troubled man*
965   Upon his compleint, when he first bigan
To tel his ladi, when he gan declare
His hidde sorois and his evel fare   *foul*
That at his hert constreyned him so sore,
Th'effecte of which was this withoute more:

970   "Princes of iouthe and flour of gentilesse,   *Princess*
Ensaumple of vertue, ground of curtesie,
Of beauté rote, quene and eke maistres
To al women hou thei shul hem gie,   *rule*
And sothefast myrrour to exemplifie
975   The righte wei of port and womanhed,
What shal I sai of merci taketh hede:

"Biseching first unto youre heigh nobles,
With quaking hert of myn inward drede,
Of grace and pité and nought of rightwisnes,
980   Of verrai routhe, to helpen in this nede.
That is to saie, O wel of goodlihed,   *source*
That I ne recch, though ye do me deie,   *do not care*
So ye list first to heren what I saie.   *desire*

"The dredful stroke, the grete force and myght
985   Of god Cupide that no man mai rebel,
So inwardli thurughout myn herte right
Ipersid hath that I ne mai concele
Myn hidde wound, ne I ne may apele   *appeal*
Unto no grettir: this myghti god so fast   *greater*
990   You to serve hath bound me to my last,   *my death*

"That hert and al withoute strife ar yolde   *surrendered*
For life or deth to youre servise alone,
Right as the goddes myghti Venus would.
Toforne hir mekeli when I made my mone,   *lament*
995   She me constreyned, without chaunge, anone   *charged*
To youre servise, and never forto feyne,
Whereso yow list to do me ease or peyne.

"So that I can nothing but merci crie
Of yow my ladi, and chaungen for no nwe,   *From; no new [lady]*
1000   That ye list goodeli tofore I deyghe,   *will graciously; die*
Of verrey routhe opon my peynes rwe.   *[Out] of genuine compassion*
For be my trouthe, and ye the sothe knwe
What is the cause of myn adversité,
On my distres ye would have pité.

1005   "For unto yow trwe and eke secré
I wole be found to serve as I best can.
And therwithal as lowli in ich degré
To yow allone, as evir yit was man
Unto his ladi, from the tyme I gan,
1010   And shal so forthe, withouten eny slouthe
Whiles that I lyve, bi god and be my trouthe.

"For levyr I had to deien sodeinli   *For rather [would]*
Than yow offend in any maner wise,
And suffre peynes inward priveli
1015   Than my servise ye shuld as nou despise.
For I right nought wil asken in no wise
But for youre servaunt ye would me accepte,
And whan I trespace, goodli me correcte,

"And forto graunt of merci this praier:
1020   Oonli of grace and womanli peté,   *Exclusively*
Fro dai to dai, that I myghte lere   *learn*
Yow forto please, and therwithal that ye,
When I do mys, list for to teche me
In youre servyse hou that I mai amende
1025   From hensforthe and nevyr yow offende.

"For unto me it doth inough suffise
That for youre man ye would me reseyve   *receive*
Fulli to ben, as you list devyse,
And as ferforthe my wittes con conceyve,   *inasmuch as*
1030   And therewithal, lich as ye perseyve   *besides, just as*
That I be trwe, to guerdone me of grace,   *repay*
Or ellis to punyssh aftir my trespace.

    "And if so be that I mai not atteyne
    Unto your merci, yit graunteth atte lest
1035 In your service, for al my wo and peyne,
    That I mai deighen aftir my bihest.
    This is al and som the fine of my request: *totality*
    Othir with merci your servant forto save   *Either*
    Or merciles that I mai be grave."   *buried*

1040 And whan this benygne of hir entent trwe
    Conceyved hath the compleint of this man,
    Right as the fressh rodi rose nwe
    Of hir coloure to wexin she bigan;
    Hir bloode astonyed so from hir hert it ran
1045 Into hir face, of femynynité:
    Thurugh honest drede abaisshed so was she

    And humbelé she gan hir eighen cast
    Towardis him of hir benygnyté,
    So that no woord bi hir lippes past
1050 For hast ne drede, merci nor pité.
    For so demeyned she was in honesté   *guided*
    That unavised nothing hir astert,   *escaped [her lips]*
    So mych of reson was compast in hir hert.

    Til at the last of routhe she did abraide,   *move*
1055 When she his trouthe and menyng dide fele,
    And unto him ful goodli spake and seide:
    "Of youre behest and of your menyng wele,
    And youre servise so feithful everedel,
    Which unto me so lowli now ye offre,
1060 With al my hert I thanke yow of youre profir,   *proposal*

    "That for as mych as youre entent is sette
    Oonli in vertu, ibridelid under drede,   *Exclusively; bridled*
    Ye most of right nedis fare the bette
    Of youre request and the bettir spede.
1065 But as for me, I mai of womanhede
    No ferthir graunt to you in myn entent
    Thanne as my ladi Venus wil assent.

    "For she wele knowith I am not at my laarge
    To done right nought but bi hir ordinaunce:
1070 So am I bound undir hir dredful charge
    Hir lust to obey withoute variaunce.   *will*
    But for my part so it be plesaunce
    Unto the goddes, for trouthe in your emprise,   *undertaking*
    I yow accepte fulli to my servyse.

1075   "For she myn hert hath in subjeccioun
        Which holi is youres and never shal repent,
        In thought nor dede, in myn eleccioun: *by my free choice*
        Witnes on Venus that knoweth myn entent
        Fulli to obei hir dome and jugement,   *decision*
1080   So as hir lust disposen and ordeyne,   *it pleases her*
        Right as she knoweth the trouth of us tweyne.   *two*

        "For unto the time that Venus list provyde
        To shape a wai for oure hertis ease,
        Bothe ye and I mekeli most abide
1085   To take agré and not of oure disease   *bear graciously*
        To grucch agein, til she list to appese   *grumble against*
        Oure hidde wo, so inli that constreyneth
        From dai to day and oure hertes peyneth.

        "For in abiding of wo and al affray,   *fear*
1090   Whoso can suffre is founden remedie;
        And for the best ful oft is made delay,
        Er men be heled of hir maladie.
        Wherfore as Venus list this mater to guie   *rule*
        Late us agreen and take al for the best,
1095   Til her list set oure hertes bothe at rest.

        "For she it is that bindeth and can constreyne
        Hertes in oon, this fortunate planete,
        And can relesen lovers of her peyne,
        To turne fulli hir bitter into swete.
1100   Nou blisful goddes, doun fro thi sterri sete   *starry dwelling*
        Us to fortune caste your stremes shene,
        Like as ye cnow that we trouthe mene."

        And therwithal, as I myn eyghen cast
        Forto perceive the maner of these twein,
1105   Tofore the goddes mekeli as thei past,
        Me thought I saw with a golden cheyne
        Venus anon enbracen and constrein
        Her bothe hertes in oon forto persever   *remain constant*
        Whiles that thei live and never to dessever.   *separate*

1110   Saiyng right thus with a benygne chere:
        "Sith it is so ye ben undir my myght,
        Mi wille is this, that ye my daughter dere
        Fulli accepte this man as hit is right,
        Unto your grace anon here in my sight,
1115   That ever hath ben so louli you to serve:
        It is goode skil your thank that he deserve.   *reasonable*

"Your honour save and eke your womanhed   *intact (assured)*
Him to cherissen it sittith you right wele,   *suits*
Sith he is bound under hope and drede
1120   Amyd my cheyne that maked is of stele.
Ye must of merci shape that he fele
In you som grace for his long servise,
And that in hast, like as I shal devyse.

"This is to sein, that ye taken hede
1125   Hou he to you most faithful is and trwe
Of al your servauntis, and nothing for his mede   *not for his compensation*
Of you ne askith but that ye on him rwe;   *except that*
For he hathe woid to chaunge for no nwe,   *vowed*
For life nor deth, for joye ne for peyne:
1130   Ay to ben yours, so as ye list ordeyne.   *Always*

"Wherfore ye must, or ellis it were wrong,
Unto your grace fulli hym receyve
In my presence, bicause he hath so long
Holli ben youres, as ye may conceyve,
1135   That from youre merci nou if ye him weyve   *turn aside*
I wil myself recorden cruelté   *declare*
In youre persone, and gret lak of pité.

"Late him for trouth then finde trouth agein;
For long service guerdone him with grace,
1140   And lateth pité weie doun his pein.   *let*
For tyme is nou daunger to arace
Out of youre hert and merci in to pace;
And love for love woulde wele biseme   *be fitting*
To geve agein, and this I pleinli deme.   *command*

1145   "And as for him I wil bene his borow   *guarantor*
Of lowlihed and bisé attendaunce: *diligent*
Hou he shal bene, both at eve and morou,
Ful diligent to don his observaunce,
And ever awayting you to do plesaunce.
1150   Wherfore, my sone, list and take hede
Fulli to obey as I shal thee rede.

"And first of al my wil is that thou be
Feithful in hert and constant as a walle,
Trwe, humble and meke, and therewithal secré,
1155   Withoute chaunge in parti or in al.
And for no turment that thee fallen shal,
Tempest thee not but ever in stidfastnes   *Anguish*
Rote thin hert and voide doublenes.   *Root*

1160
"And forthermore have in reverence
Thes women al for thi ladi sake,   *Women in general*
And suffre never that men do them offence,   *tolerate*
For love of oon; but evermore undirtake
Hem to defend, whether thei slepe or wake,
And ay be redi to holden champartie   *hold your own*
1165   With alle tho that to hem have envie.

"Be curteis ay and lowli of thi spech
To riche and poure ai fressh and welbesein,   *ever; nice-looking*
And ever bisie, weies forto sech   *search*
All trwe lovers to relese of her peyne,
1170   Sith thou art oon; and of no wight have disdein,
For love hath pouer hertis forto daunt;
And never for cherisshing thee to mych avaunte.   *boast*

"Be lusti eke, devoid of al tristesse,   *melancholy*
And take no thought but ever be jocond,   *joyous*
1175   And nought to pensif for non hevynes;
And with thi gladnes let sadnes ay be found;   *gravity also*
When wo approcheth let myrth most habound,   *overflow*
As manhod axeth; and though thou fele smert,   *demands*
Lat not to manie knowen of thin hert.

1180   "And al vertues biseli thou sue,   *pursue*
Vices eschew for the love of oon;
And for no tales thin herte not remue: *block*
Woorde is but winde that shal sone overgon.   *pass away*
Whatever thou here be doumb as eny ston,   *hear*
1185   And to answere to sone not thee delite,   *too soon*
For here she standeth that al this shal thee quite.   *requite*

"And where thou be absent or in presence,   *whether*
None othirs beauté lat in thin herte myne,   *break into (undermine)*
Sith I have hir gyve of beauté excellence
1190   Above al othir in vertue forto shine;
And thenk that in fire hou men ar wont to fyne   *refine*
This purid gold, to put it in assay:
So thee to preve, thou ert put in delay.

"But tyme shal come thou shalt for thi sufferaunce
1195   Be wele apaide and take for thi mede   *sufficiently paid; reward*
Thi lives joy and al thi suffisaunce,
So that goode hope alway thi bridel lede.
Lat no dispeire hindir thee with drede,
But ay thi trust opon hir merci ground,
1200   Sith noon but she may thi sores sound.   *heal*

"Eche houre and tyme, weke, dai and yere,   *weak*
Be iliche feithful and varie not for lite;   *constantly; for some small thing*
Abide awhile and than of thi desire
The time neigheth that shal thee most delite.
1205 And lete no sorou in thin herte bite   *bite*
For no differring, sith thou shalt for thi mede   *reward*
Rejoise in pees the floure of womanhede.

"Thenk hou she is this worldis sonne and light,
The sterre of beauté, flour eke of fairnes,
1210 Bothe crop and rote, and eke the rubie bright
Hertes to glade itroubled with derknes,
And hou I have made hir thin hertes emperesse.
Be glad therfore to be undir hir bonde.
Nou come nere, doughter, and take him by the hond,

1215 "Unto this fyne that after al the showres   *end; hardships*
Of his turment, he mai be glad and light
Whan thurugh youre grace ye take him to be youres
For evermore anon here in my syght.
And eeke also I wil, as it is ryght
1220 Withoute more his langour forto lisse,   *sorrow to assuage*
In my presence anon that ye him kisse:

"That here mai be of al youre olde smertis
A ful relese undir joy assured;
And that oo lok be of youre bothe hertes   *one lock*
1225 Shet with my key of gold so wel depured,   *purified*
Oonli in signe that ye have recured   *Specially; acquired*
Youre hole desire here in this holi place,
Within my temple nou in the yere of grace.

"Eternalli, be bonde of assuraunce,
1230 The cnott is knytt, which mai not ben unbound,
That al the goddis of this alliaunce,   *as regards this alliance*
Saturne and Jove and Mars, as it is founde,
And eke Cupide that first you dide wounde,   *Cupid who*
Shal bere record and overmore be wreke   *moreover be avenged*
1235 On which of you his trouthe first dothe breke,

"So that bi aspectes of hir ferse lokes,   *bearing; fierce appearance*
Withoute merci shal falle the vengeaunce
Forto be raced clene out of my bokes,   *erased*
On which of yow be founde variaunce.
1240 Therfore atones setteth your plesauns   *together (once and for all)*
Fulli to ben, while ye have life and mynd,
Of oon accord unto youre lyves ende,

	"That if the spirit of nufangilnes	*fondness for novelty*
	In any wise youre hertis would assaile	*manner; assail*
1245	To meve or stir to bring in doubilnes	
	Upon your trouthe to given a bataile,	*Against; to provoke*
	Late not youre corage ne youre force fail,	
	Ne non assautes you flitten or remeve:	*[make you] flee or abandon*
	For unassaied men may no trouthe preve.	*untried; prove*

1250	"For white is whitter if it be set bi blak,	
	And swete is swettir eftir bitternes,	
	And falshode ever is drive and put abak	
	Where trouthe is rotid withoute doubilnes.	*rooted (fixed)*
	Withoute prefe may be no sikirnes	*proof; certainty*
1255	Of love or hate; and therfor of yow too	
	Shal love be more, that it was bought with wo.	*[for the reason] that*

	"As evere thing is had more in deinté,	*held more precious*
	And more of pris when it is dere bought;	*dearly*
	And eke that love stond more in sureté	*confidently*
1260	When it tofore with peyne, wo and thought	*before*
	Conquerid was, first when it was sought;	
	And evere conquest hath his excellens	
	In his pursuite as he fint resistence:	

	"And so to yow more sote and agreable	*sweet*
1265	Shal love be found — I do you plein assure —	
	Withoute grucching that ye were suffrable,	*[in] that; capable of enduring suffering*
	So low, so meke, so pacientli t'endure,	
	That al atones I shal nou do my cure	*at once*
	For nou and ever your hertis so to bynd,	
1270	That nought but deth shal the knot unbynd.	

	"Nou in this mater what shuld I lengir dwel?	*longer dwell*
	Cometh at ones and do as I have seide.	
	And first, my doughter, that bene of bounté wele,	*virtue [the] wellspring*
	In hert and thought be glad and wele apaied	*contented*
1275	To done him grace that hath, and shal, obeid	
	Youre lustes ever; and I wole for his sake	*wishes*
	Of trouthe to yow be bounde and undertake."	

	And so forthwith in presence as thei stonde	*at once in the assembly*
	Tofore the goddes, this ladi faire and wele	
1280	Hir humble servaunt toke goodli bi the honde,	
	As he toforne here mekeli did knele,	
	And kissed him after, fulfillyng everedele	
	Fro point to point in ful tristi wise,	*in faithful manner*
	As ye toforne have Venus herd devyse.	

1285   Thus is this man to joy and al plesaunce
        From hevynes and from his peynes old
        Ful reconsiled, and hath ful suffisaunce   *satisfaction*
        Of hir that ever mente wel and would:
        And in goode faith, thogh I telle shuld
1290   The inward myrthe that dide hir hertis brace,   *embrace*
        For al my life it were to lit a space.   *too small*

        For he hathe wonne hir that he loveth best,
        And she to grace hathe take him of pité;
        And thus her hertis bethe bothe set in rest,
1295   Withouten chaunge or mutabilité,
        And Venus hath of hir benygneté
        Confermed all (what shal I lenger tarie?)   *why shall I further delay?*
        This tweyn in oon, and nevere forto varie:

        That for the joy in the temple aboute
1300   Of this accord, bi gret solempnyté,
        Was laude and honoure within and withoute
        Geve unto Venus and to the deité
        Of god Cupide, so that Caliopé
        And al hir sustren in hir armonye   *act of singing (harmony)*
1305   Sone with her song the goddes magnyfie.   *Immediately*

        And al at ones with notes loude and sharpe
        Thei did her honour and her reverence,
        And Orpheus among hem with his harp
        Gan strengis touch with his diligence,   *strike*
1310   And Amphioun that hathe such excellence
        Of musike ay dide his bisynes   *ever*
        To please and queme Venus the goddes,   *gratify*

        Oonli for cause of the affinité   *Solely*
        Betwix these twoo not likli to dessevere.
1315   And evere lover of lough and heigh degré   *low and high*
        Gan Venus pray: fro thensforth and ever
        That hool of hem the love may persevere,   *together their love*
        Withouten ende in suche plite as thei gonne,   *danger as they undertake*
        And more encrese that it of hard was wonne.   *[in] that*

1320   And so the goddes, hering this request,
        As she that knew the clene entencioun
        Of bothe hem tweyne, hath made a ful bihest:
        Perpetuelli, by confirmacioun,
        Whiles that thei lyve, of oon affeccioun
1325   Thei shal endure (ther is no more to sein)
        That neither shal have mater to compleyne.

"So ferforth ever in oure eternal se   *Thus far; heavenly abode*
The goddes have, in oure presscience,   *foresight*
Fulli devysed thurugh hir deité,   *Fully chosen*
1330   And holi concludid bi hir influence,   *special powers*
That thurugh hir myght and juste providence
The love of hem, bi grace and eke fortune,
Withoute chaunge shal ever in oon contune."   *continue*

Of whiche graunt, the tempil enviroun,   *throughout*
1335   Thurugh heigh confort of hem that were present,
Anone was gone with a melodius sowne,[1]
In name of tho that trouth in love ment,   *true love intended (strove for)*
A ballade nwe in ful goode entent
Tofore the goddes with notes loude and clere,   *Before the goddess*
1340   Singyng right thus anon as ye shal here:

"Fairest of sterres that with youre persant light   *piercing*
And with the cherisshing of youre stremes clere
Causen in love hertes to ben light,
Oonli thurugh shynyng of youre glade spere: *Only*
1345   Nou laude and pris, O Venus, ladi dere,   *praise and glory*
Be to your name, that have withoute synne
This man fortuned his ladi forto wynne.

"Willi planet, O Esperus so bright,   *Benign (Propitious)*
That woful hertes can appese and sterre,   *guide (steer)*
1350   And ever ar redi thurugh your grace and myght
To help al tho that bie love so dere,   *those who purchase*
And have power hertis to set on fire:
Honor to yow of all that bene hereinne,   *from all*
That have this man his ladi made to wynne.

1355   "O myghti goddes, daister after nyght,   *morning star*
Glading the morou whan ye done appere,
To voide derknes thurugh fresshnes of your sight,
Oonli with twinkeling of youre plesaunt chere: *Simply*
To you we thank, lovers that ben here,
1360   That ye this man — and never forto twyn —
Fortuned have his ladi forto wynne."

And with the noise and hevenli melodie
Which that thei made in her armonye
Thurughoute the temple, for this manes sake,

---

[1] Lines 1334–36: *For which grant, throughout the temple, / Owing to the great relief of those present, / At once [a new ballad] was begun with a melodious sound*

1365	Oute of my slepe anone I did awake,	
	And for astonied knwe as tho no rede.	*in bewilderment was at a loss*
	For sodein chaunge, oppressid so with drede,	
	Me thought I was cast as in a traunce:	
	So clene away was tho my remembraunce	
1370	Of al my dreme, wherof gret thought and wo	
	I hade in hert and nyst what was to do,	*knew not*
	For hevynes that I hade lost the sight	
	Of hir that I all the longe nyght	
	Had dremed of in myn avisioun.	*dream vision*
1375	Whereof I made gret lamentacioun	
	Bicause I had never in my life aforne	*previously*
	Sein none so faire, fro time that I was borne;	
	For love of whome, so as I can endite,	
	I purpose here to maken and to write	
1380	A litil tretis and a processe make	*discourse; narrative*
	In pris of women, oonli for hir sake,	
	Hem to comende as it is skil and right,	
	For here goodnes, with al my fulle myght:	
	Praying to hir that is so bounteous,	
1385	So ful of vertue and so gracious	
	Of womanhed and merciful pité,	
	This simpil tretis forto take in gré	*simple poem; graciously*
	Til I have leiser unto hir heigh renoun	
	Forto expoune my forseid visioun,	*interpret; aforesaid*
1390	And tel in plein the significaunce,	
	So as it cometh to my remembraunce,	
	So that herafter my ladi may it loke.	
	Nou go thi wai, thou litel rude boke,	*simple (dull-witted)*
	To hir presence, as I thee comaund,	
1395	And first of al thou me recomaund	
	Unto hir and to hir excellence,	
	And prai to hir that it be noon offence	
	If eny woorde in thee be myssaide,	*mispoken*
	Biseching hir she be not evel apaied;	*dissatisfied*
1400	For as hir list I wil thee efte correcte,	*desires; after*
	When that hir liketh againward thee directe:	*directs you back [to me]*
	I mene that benygne and goodli of hir face.	
	Nou go thi way and put thee in hir grace.	

EXPLANATORY NOTES

ABBREVIATIONS: *BD*: Chaucer, *Book of the Duchess*; *CA*: Gower, *Confessio Amantis*; *CT*: Chaucer, *Canterbury Tales*; *G*: Cambridge, University Library, MS Gg.4.27; *HF*: Chaucer, *House of Fame*; *LGW*: Chaucer, *Legend of Good Women*; *MED*: *Middle English Dictionary*; *Metam.*: Ovid, *Metamorphoses*; *OED*: *Oxford English Dictionary*; *PF*: Chaucer, *Parliament of Fowls*; *RR*: Chaucer, *Romaunt of the Rose*; *S*: London, British Library, MS Additional 16165; *T*: Oxford, Bodleian Library, MS Tanner 346 (base-text for this edition); *TC*: Chaucer, *Troilus and Criseyde*; *TG*: Lydgate, *Temple of Glas*; **Whiting**: Whiting, *Proverbs, Sentences, and Proverbial Phrases*.

1–3   The cause of the narrator's malady is not identified, but his symptoms are those of a man driven to bed by lovesickness. The idea has origins in *RR*, lines 2553–64, and, going back further, in Ovid's *Amores* 1.2.1–4. Lydgate would have had in mind the insomniac dreamer-poet, the cause of whose sleeplessness is not explained in *BD* and *HF*, and he was likely also familiar with antecedents in the French tradition which Chaucer adapted and deviated from (see Windeatt, *Chaucer's Dream Poetry*). Only at the end of *TG* (lines 1375–1403) does the poet identify himself as an abject lover (unlike Chaucer's narrators), though the nature of his situation remains ambiguous. The confessional tone struck by the poem's opening lines is carried through in the lovers' complaints within the dream.

1   *For thought, constreint, and grevous hevines*. Norton-Smith hears an echo of *RR*, line 308: "For sorowe, thought, and gret distresse" (*John Lydgate: Poems*, p. 179).

3   *this othir nyght*. Setting fictional events within a bedchamber in a recent, pseudo-autobiographical past produces a general sense of intimacy, individuality, and gossipy familiarity. Norton-Smith finds the same phrase in *BD*, line 45 (*John Lydgate: Poems*, p. 180). But in Chaucer the phrase means "this second night," referring to the protagonist's sleeplessness, thereby setting up the dreamer's awakening at twelve bells on the third day. Here, in *TG*, the sense may simply imply "recently."

4–7   *Whan that Lucina . . . the nwe yere*. The poet goes to bed when the moon (*Lucina*) is in conjunction with the sun (*Phebus*); but as it is December, these planets would have entered Capricorn, not Aquarius. "The astronomy is literary, not scientific. Lydgate purposely avoids any tradition of precise dating which would postulate a real situation" (*TG*, ed. Norton-Smith, p. 180). Others have nevertheless felt that such circumstantial detail provokes rather than frustrates the search for historical reference. In his edition of the poem,

Schick (*TG*, p. cxiv) makes attempts at dating the poem on the basis of the astronomical signs.

6   *Amyd Decembre.* The dream in *HF*, lines 111–12, occurs on 10 December.

7   *kalendes.* Referring either to dates on the calendar reckoned back as far as to the middle of the current month from the first of the following month (*MED* 1c), or perhaps more generally to a sense of expectancy around this time (*MED* 2). Either way, the poet seems to be awaiting some bright change even amidst dark December, and this anticipates a pattern of light/dark imagery later in the poem, on which see the explanatory note to lines 20-29.

8   *And derk Diane, ihorned.* Diane, goddess of chastity, and another name for the moon (also known as Cynthea, Latona, and Lucina). The reference is to the crescent moon, perceived as though it had horns. There may be an implied mythological and astrological juxtaposition with Venus, goddess of love, who rules inside the dream vision. Here the horned headpiece suggests aristocratic fashion, not cuckoldry.

14   *sodein dedeli slepe.* Restlessness followed by a swift and decisive fall into sleep is conventionally Chaucerian; compare *BD*, line 272, *HF*, line 114, and *PF*, line 94.

16   *temple of glas.* Lydgate's description of this architectural marvel (surrounded by wilderness or wasteland; set upon an icy foundation; containing statues and murals; populated by gods and supplicants) owes much to Chaucer's Temple of Glass (*HF*, lines 119–488), where glass implies mirrors, and something to his Castle of Fame (e.g., line 1130), with its foundation of ice. Another precedent is Chaucer's "temple of bras" in *PF*, line 231, which houses Priapus, Venus, and Cupid, among other ministers and devotees of love, and which is engraved with stories of many famous lovers. Lydgate's scribes or rubricators must have had this temple on their minds when they gave *TG* the title *The Temple of Bras* in two manuscripts (see *TG*, ed. Schick, p. xvii). Finally, another relevant Temple of Venus features in Chaucer's Knight's Tale, *CT* I(A)1918–66.

20–29   *And as I did approche....* The splendor of the place evokes the intensity of love; see *TC* 2.862–65 for a comparison of the sun and love. Ebin, *John Lydgate*, p. 30, argues that the "system of light and dark images, which link the various segments of the poem, provide the vehicle for successive redefinitions of love." Davidoff, *Beginning Well*, pp. 135–46, also addresses the contrastive effects of light and darkness and argues that the dreamer's experience is one of illumination and insight occurring in a place of imaginative splendor. By contrast, Crockett, in "Venus Unveiled," pp. 73–74, construes the dazzling scene as an indictment of the narrator's moral blindness.

32   *Titan.* This refers to the Titan sun god Helios, father of Phaethon, not the Olympian sun god Phoebus Apollo (e.g., line 4), twin of Diana (line 8).

39   *wiket.* The gate recalls similar narrow passageways through which other voyeuristic poets enter into secret, restricted, or sanctified spaces; compare *RR*, lines 528–30, and *HF*, line 477. A reader familiar with Chaucer is destined to

recall the garden "wyket" that is an important architectural feature of The Merchant's Tale, as well; for indeed, as if in imitation of the furtiveness of Damian (*CT* IV[E]2151–54), Lydgate's dreamer enters through the wicket suspiciously "fast," and in his intrusion into private affairs he is not unlike the adulterous lover who trespasses on another man's property and has his way with his wife. Of course, *TG* is a much more decorous affair than that retailed in The Merchant's Tale. Nevertheless, as becomes clear by the end of *TG*, Lydgate's dreamer-poet aspires to a similar role in a love triangle (or rather, rectangle), though he is apparently doomed to be an observer rather than a participant. On the voyeuristic poet in other late medieval love poems, see Spearing, *Medieval Poet as Voyeur*.

44–142   *I saughe depeynt opon everé wal.* . . . An inscription and tableau of the legend of Dido and Aeneas is the principal feature of the Temple of Glass in *HF*, lines 151–467; the walls of the Temple of Venus in The Knight's Tale, *CT* I(A) 1918–66, portray the symptoms of lovesickness, personified behaviors, and a few famous lovers. *PF*, lines 284–94, with its panoply of lovers, may lie behind the depiction of *ful many a faire image / Of sondri lovers* in *TG* (lines 95-96). Lydgate refers to most of the legendary lovers listed there (Dido and Aeneas, Isolde and Tristan, Thisbe and Piramus, Paris and Helen, Polyxena and Achilles), picturing many more besides whose tales are told elsewhere by Chaucer. Indeed, the list in *TG* reads like an homage to Chaucerian *auctoritas* in a manner similar to Chaucer's own Introduction to The Man of Law's Tale, *CT* II(B^1) 57–76, impressing upon readers that Chaucer is the inimitable poet who "hath toold of loveris up and doun" (*CT* II[B^1]53). *TG* as it stands in T suggests other ways in which Chaucer's secular and vernacular authority was transmitted, specifically in its emulation of Chaucer's compilatory *LGW* (on which see the discussion of Tanner in Lerer's *Chaucer and His Readers*, pp. 57–84). But the similarities are designed not to suggest literary sources, but rather shared poetic spaces shaped for a literate readership well sophisticated by the delights of courtly poetry.

46–47   *lich as thei were of age . . . aftir thei were trwe.* The reference to "age" is unclear and may indicate that the figures are either positioned in order of their physical age or, more likely, represented as young adults (i.e., come of age); and "trwe" may refer to fidelity or a true likeness. Whatever the sense of these lines, the catalogue of lovers apparently does not reproduce any such order in its pictorial arrangement.

52–53   *Venus . . . fleting in the se.* The familiar iconography of the Marine Venus, or Venus *anadyomene*, is only one of several forms she takes in *TG*. Chaucer offers his own visual description of the floating Venus in The Knight's Tale, *CT* I(A)1955–66, and *HF*, lines 131–37; see Twycross, *Medieval Anadyomene*. Crockett notes that according to medieval mythographers this image is "emblematic of concupiscence" ("Venus Unveiled," p. 80, citing *Fulgentius the Mythographer* 2.1 [trans. Whitbread, pp. 66–67]). But Lydgate elsewhere construes the image as a sign of "þe trowble and aduersite / Þat is in Loue, and his stormy lawe, / Whiche is beset with many sturdy wawe, / Now calm, now rowe, who-so takethþ hede, / And hope assailled ay with sodeyn drede" (*Troy Book* 2.2544–48), and this "factual" account of desire is compatible with *TG*. On the various Venuses who appear in Lydgate's works see Tinkle, *Medieval Venuses and Cupids*, pp. 129–35 and 154–59, who observes that in *TG* alone Venus is repeatedly reinterpreted — as mythological, astral, natural, carnal, or courtly — and cannot be reduced to a single meaning. Bianco makes a similar observation in "New Perspectives," pp. 109–14, noting that Venus takes the form of "a painting, a statue, a planet or a living, speaking advisor."

55–61   Queen Dido of Carthage, expressing great anguish over Aeneas' deception, pictured just before she ends her life. Derived from Virgil's *Aeneid* 4, her complaint was elaborated in Ovid's *Heroides* 7. Dido's tragedy figures in *HF*, lines 219–426, and *LGW*, lines 924–1367, and Gower tells the tale in *CA* 4.77–142 to illustrate Aeneas' "sloth" in love. Like Chaucer and Gower, Lydgate gives Dido the benefit of a pathetic treatment: the poets do not follow the austere mythographic tradition that construed Aeneas' flight from Carthage as noble resistance to sexual temptation (see Crockett, "Venus Unveiled," p. 75), but rather align their sympathies with the abandoned heroine.

62–63   Medea, even after helping her husband Jason to accomplish various heroic deeds, is abandoned by him for another woman, as recounted in Ovid's *Heroides* 12 and *Metam.* 7. Compare *LGW*, lines 1368–1679, and CA 5.3247–4222. Lydgate tells the story at length in Book 1 of *Troy Book*.

64–65   Venus' passion for Adonis (*Addoun*), slain by a boar in the forest, is recounted in *Metam.* 10. Mentioned in Chaucer's Knight's Tale, *CT* I(A)224, and *TC* 3.720–21.

67–69   Penelope, who faithfully awaits the return of her husband Ulysses from Troy, is regularly considered alongside Alcestis (who is next described in *TG*) as an exemplary true wife. See the Introduction to The Man of Law's Tale, *CT* II(B^1)75, The Franklin's Tale, *CT* V(F)1442–43, and *TC* 5.1778. Gower relates the story in *CA* 4.147–233, where Ulysses is blamed for tardiness; and Penelope is grouped together with Lucrece, Alcestis, and Alcyone as one of Four Noble Wives in *CA* 8.2621–56. Although in The Franklin's Tale Chaucer cites "Omer" (Homer's *Odyssey*) as the source of the story of Penelope and Ulysses, medieval poets knew it from Ovid's *Heroides* 1.

70–74   Queen Alcestis, transformed into a daisy in tribute to her self-sacrificing love for her husband Admetus, is the heroine of *LGW*, F Prologue, lines 510–16, and the subject of *CA* 7.1917–43. The story was passed down in numerous medieval translations; see *Fulgentius the Mythographer*, 1.22 (trans. Whitbread, pp. 62–63).

75–76   Griselda's *innocence, mekenes,* and *pacience* are exemplified in her endurance of the extreme tests set by her husband Walter. Lydgate would have known the story from Chaucer's Clerk's Tale, but it circulated widely in various languages throughout medieval Europe from tellings of the tale by Boccaccio and Petrarch; see Bronfman, *Chaucer's Clerk's Tale*.

77–79   Isolde is the legendary lover of Tristan, nephew to her husband King Mark of Cornwall. Their tragic and illicit affair is transmitted in several medieval versions; see Eisner, *Tristan Legend*. The lovers are mentioned among other figures adorning the walls of the Temple of Brass in *PF*, line 290, and they are found in *CA* 6.471–75. Evidently, the list of "trwe" (line 47) lovers painted on the wall does not discriminate between faithful wives (Penelope, Alcestis, and Griselda) and adulterers (Isolde), which suggests that the standard of truth operating here is not conformity to the social institution of marriage: the poem will go on to enlarge on the idea that sentimental love is a law unto itself. Moreover, forbidden or clandestine love has its own powerful attractions in the poem.

80–81   The unhappy tale of Piramus and Thisbe (*Tesbie*), who were prohibited from loving by their parents and became a double suicide, is derived from *Metam.* 4. Related in *LGW*, lines 706–923, and *CA* 3.1331–1494.

82–85   Duke Theseus of Athens vanquished the Minotaur. Like Chaucer's Knight, the narrator fails to mention the love intrigue which forms the context of the duke's heroics: Ariadne, who came to his assistance in figuring out how to negotiate the Cretan labyrinth, was famously dumped by Theseus. The original story is recounted in Ovid's *Heroides* 10 and *Metam.* 7 –8. Theseus' treachery is the subject of *LGW*, lines 1886–2227. *CA* 5.5231–5493 also gives the history including Theseus' "unkindness" towards Ariadne. Theseus is the only one among other celebrated lovers in Lydgate who, in other contexts, is a perpetrator rather than a victim. Here, as in Chaucer's Knight's Tale, he is simply a worthy leader who destroyed the Minotaur.

83   *amyd the hous*. The labyrinth is commonly referred to as the house of Daedalus ("Domus Dedaly," *HF*, line 1920) or "labyrinthus" as in *Aeneid* 5.588. See John Fyler's note, *Riverside Chaucer*, p. 989n1920–21, which notes also Higden's *Polychronicon* ("laborintus," "Dedalus hous") and Chaucer's *Boece* 3.pr12.156, where "hous of dedalus" is glossed "domus dedaly." See also *Metam.* 8.156–58. Chaucer describes the maze in *LGW* 2012–14.

86–90   Phyllis is betrayed by Demophon, son of Duke Theseus, and upon committing suicide she is transformed into a hazelnut tree; but her metamorphosis is not mentioned in Lydgate's brief summary. The source is Ovid's *Heroides* 2 and *Remedia Amoris*, lines 591–604. Her story is related in *LGW*, lines 2394–561, and, briefly, in *HF*, lines 388–96. *CA* 4.731–878 is probably the source of Lydgate's "filbert" (previously identified as an almond tree, or unspecified, in classical sources; see *TG*, ed. Schick, pp. 75–76).

92–93   Paris "won" or abducted Helen from her husband, the Spartan Menelaus, and took her back to Troy. The escapade was known chiefly from *Heroides* 16–17. The lovers are painted on the walls of Chaucer's Temple of Brass, *PF*, lines 290–91, and their story is essential background information in *TC* 1.57–63. Lydgate will go on to relate the full history of the abduction in the second book of *Troy Book*.

94–95   Achilles is slain in the temple where he was set to marry Polixena (*Policene*), a tragic event given brief mention in *BD*, lines 1069–71; the lovers also appear on the walls of the brass temple in *PF*, line 290. Chaucer acknowledges his source as Dares' *De excidio Troiae historia*, but medieval poets equally depended on Benoît de Sainte-Maure's *Roman de Troie*, besides other chroniclers of Troy.

97–99   Philomena is raped and has her tongue cut out by Tereus, but she is able to communicate her ordeal to her sister Procne (*Progne*, wife of Tereus) using a tapestry; the sisters metamorphose into birds when Tereus attempts to kill them. *Metam.* 6.424–605 is the source. Chaucer alludes to the sisters in *TC* 2.64–70 and tells a partial story in *LGW*, lines 2228–2393. For the full story, see *CA* 5.5551–6047.

100   *Sabyns*. Sabines are "a race of ancient Italy who inhabited the central region of the Apennines" (*OED*). Legend holds that the Sabine women were raped by and forced to intermarry with the Romans. Their tragic history of sexual victimization at the hands of Romans is no doubt the reason the Sabines are mentioned alongside Lucretia (as they are in Livy's *History of Rome* 1 and in Dante's *Paradiso* 6), on which more below.

101   The Roman Lucretia (*Lucresse*), after she was raped by Sextus Tarquinius, committed suicide to defend her honor and that of her husband Collatinus. The "fest of Lucresse" refers to the Regifugium ("Flight of the King" on 24 February), a festival held in commemoration of the expulsion of the last Roman king, Tarquinius Superbus, who was forced to flee Rome because his son Sextus so violated Lucretia. As Ovid explains in *Fasti* 2.685–852, Lucretia's death inspired Brutus to take up arms against King Tarquinius. Therefore, the Sabines who observe the feast day of Lucretia are mourning the sexual exploitation of their ancestors, but also celebrating a political watershed — the advent of Roman republicanism — made possible, in no small part, by the heroism of Lucretia. Lydgate speaks explicitly of the political fallout in his *Serpent of Division*, ed. MacCracken, p. 49. On the rapes of Lucretia and the Sabine women, see Livy's *History of Rome* 1. The question of the heroism of Lucretia's suicide is discussed in Augustine's *City of God*, 1.19. Chaucer recounts the legend in *LGW*, lines 1680–1885; Gower in *CA* 7.4754–5130.

102–10   *There saugh I also . . . as Chaucer tellith us*. A synopsis of the first two parts of The Knight's Tale, *CT* I(A)859–1880, in which the Theban knights Palamon and Arcite are smitten by the sight of Emily, whom they glimpse from a prison cell in Athens. They are compelled to settle their dispute in a manner decided by Theseus. Lerer observes that the summary is the longest of all the descriptions of "sondri lovers," and the only one to mention a source. Its centrality leads him to argue that the narrator is presented as a "reader" of Chaucer (Lerer, *Chaucer and His Readers*, pp. 69–70).

105   *hurt unwarli thurugh casting of an eyghe*. A motif of courtly poetry. See Chaucer's Knight's Tale, *CT* I(A)1077–97 and *TC* 2.533–36. Compare lines 231–32 and 850.

112–16	The nymph Daphne, pursued through the forest by the love-struck Phoebus Apollo, escapes the fiery passion of the sun god when she is transformed into a laurel tree. The story is derived from *Metam.* 1.452–567, and referred to in *TC* 3.726–27. Gower has a version of the fable in *CA* 3.1685–1720.
112	*arow of gold.* Compare line 445. Cupid's arrows are described in *RR*, lines 918–98.
114	*envie of the god Cupide.* According to *Metam.* 1.452–567, Cupid targets Phebus just to prove that the shafts of love are more powerful than the shafts of the sun.
117–20	Jove (or Jupiter), another promiscuous shape-changing god, took the form of a bull when he ravished Europa. The story is derived from *Metam.* 2.833–75, and referred to very briefly in *TC* 3.722–24.
121–25	Jove sleeps with Alcmene (*Almen*) by taking on the *shap* (line 122) of her husband Amphitrion, thereby conceiving Hercules. See Ovid's *Amores* 1.13.45–46 and *Metam.* 6.112. Chaucer makes passing reference to the night of sexual intrigue in *TC* 3.1428; an adaptation of the legend can be found in *CA* 2.2459–95.
126–28	Vulcan, the unattractive and aged husband of Venus, discovered his wife engaged in sexual congress with the dashing warrior god Mars. Vulcan fettered the adulterers with chains and exposed them to the other gods, but the gods were charmed by the sight of the handsome pair of lovers and only ridiculed Vulcan. The origin is *Metam.* 4.171–89 and *Ars Amatoria* 2.561–92; also transmitted in *Romance of the Rose*, lines 18061–130 and *Fulgentius the Mythographer*, 2.7 (trans. Whitbread, pp. 72–73). Chaucer refers to the incident in The Knight's Tale, *CT* I(A)2383–92, and in *A Complaint of Mars.* Gower tells the tale, in *CA* 5.635–725, as if from the perspective of the mocking gods, applying the example to jealous husbands: it is better to pretend you know nothing of your wife's infidelity than to attract slander for petty jealousy. Lydgate seems nearly as sympathetic in *Complaynt of a Loveres Lyfe*, lines 389–92 and 621–26. In another version of *TG*, Lydgate daringly capitalized on the amorality of the fable to draw an explicit comparison between the situation of Venus and that of the lady: in stanzas that replace lines 335–69 of the present edition (see explanatory notes to those lines below), the lady identifies herself as among those women who are "oppressed" no less than Venus was by her jealous husband. Lydgate may have altered these lines (or a scribe may have done so), but they only make explicit a romantic notion that is implicit elsewhere in all of the surviving versions of *TG*: erotic desire has its own natural justification that transcends the artificial constraints of legal marriage.
129–36	*Mercurie* and *Philologye.* Alluding to Martianus Capella's *Marriage of Philology and Mercury*, a fifth-century work well known to the later Middle Ages. Chaucer makes passing references to the marriage in The Merchant's Tale, *CT* IV(E)1732–37, and *HF*, line 985. Crockett thinks the juxtaposition here of Mercury and Philology with Mars and Venus generates an ironic contrast between "virtuous" and "corrupt love" ("Venus Unveiled," pp. 75–76). But

medieval love poets take much pleasure in moral equivocation, and Lydgate certainly abstains from explicit moral condemnation in *TG*. Chaucer's Wife of Bath, *CT* III(D)697–705, describes the contrary astrological influences of the planets Mercury (god of studious but boring old clerks) and Venus (goddess of lusty, youthful women). In *CA* 7.755–800 the planets are contrasted in a similarly ambivalent manner: Mercury governs bookish, idle, avaricious folk (mainly in France), while Venus governs the amorous, courteous, and pleasure-seeking (Italians).

138–42   The passage introduces the last set of painted figures and alludes to Chaucer's Squire's Tale, *CT* V(F)9–708, an unfinished romance told by "a yong Squier, / A lovyere and a lusty bacheler" (General Prologue, *CT* I[A]79–80). In it Canacee receives a gift of a magic ring, enabling her to commune with a lovelorn falcon who relates a tragic tale of betrayal. Canacee's brother receives a mechanical brass horse, but the narrative breaks off before we find out exactly how he was *oft holpen* (*TG*, line 141) by the magical gift (but see *CT* V[F]666 for the Squire's declared intention to relate the whole matter).

143–246   The focus of the dream vision now shifts from the "past perfect," in which the fates of legendary lovers have long been decided in the ancient past and are memorialized in static pictures, to the suspended "continuous present": the thousands now in the temple are *redi to complein* (line 145), and the outcomes of their cases remain undecided. This is the anxious context out of which will emerge the figure of a lady pleading her case to Venus, and even at the end of the poem the fate of the central characters remains unknown. Those awaiting an audience with Venus are like the petitioners in other courts of love (e.g., *Assembly of Ladies* and James I's *Kingis Quair*), and they are further reminiscent of the groups who come asking favors of Fame in *HF*.

147–48   *envie . . . fals Jelousie*. Schick capitalizes *envie* to give it the force of personification, partly on the authority of *RR* lines 247–48: "Envye, that never lough / Nor never wel in hir herte ferde." I mark abstract nouns as personified figures where the immediate context dictates an allegorical sense (e.g., "fals Jelousie"); capitalization is employed elsewhere, but sparingly. "Lydgate's practice seems sometimes to hover just short of personification, posing some difficulties for an editor" (*TG*, ed. Boffey, p. 33).

156   *Daunger*. Guardian of the rosebush in *RR*, lines 3015 ff., Daunger represents the lady's aloof or guarded attitude towards her suitors, dramatized later in the poem when in lines 1047–53 the lady betrays no enthusiasm for her lover. Daunger is mentioned together with Disdain in *PF*, line 136, a line which may be the source of Lydgate's.

159   *poverté*. Personified in *RR*, line 450.

175   *Riches*. Also personified in *RR*, line 1033. Compare *PF*, line 261.

179–95   *And some ther were as maydens yung of age*. The circumstances and the frank language recall Chaucer's Merchant's Tale, *CT* IV(E)1245–2418, to which Lydgate expressly alludes in the reference to the ill-matched marriage of January and May. The theme is also taken up in Chaucer's Miller's Tale, *CT* I(A)3224–30.

Another version of the complaint (as given in MSS G and S) strongly suggests that the lady would have belonged to this group of plaintiffs; see explanatory notes to lines 126–28 and 335-69. In the extenuating light of such forced alliances between impotent old men and young women, Lydgate's lovers should not have to plead very hard to justify their romantic wishes (the absorbing sentimentality of which verges at times on the anti-matrimonial in *TG*). Genuine affection — even if adulterous — is probably more noble by contrast.

182 *elde*. A personification in *RR*, line 349.

196–208 *And right anon I herd othir crie*. These others are "child oblates" who were committed at a young age by their parents or guardians to a monastery or convent. The Benedictine Rule was particularly strict in holding that oblates were bound for life to remain in their religious vocation, but the practice was (officially) obsolescent by the thirteenth century, and wherever it continued would have been controversial: as Lydgate himself observes, adult oblates learned to keep up superficial appearances. Lydgate was himself enlisted in the Benedictine monastery at Bury St. Edmunds when only a young adolescent, and he did not immediately take to the discipline (according to his own *The Testament of Dan John Lydgate* in *The Minor Poems*, ed. MacCracken), leading Schick to conclude that "Lydgate was certainly thinking of himself when he wrote those lines" (*TG*, p. lxxxviii). But the complaint was widespread, even conventional; e.g., compare *The Court of Love*, lines 1095–1136, and James I's *Kingis Quair*, lines 624–30. See de Jong, *In Samuel's Image*.

199 *That conseiles in hir tender youthe*. Perhaps referring to meddling guardians or advisers (compare *MED, counseils*), but as this is not a very satisfactory reading Schick freely emends to *constrayned*. But the original passage makes good enough sense if we take the phrase to mean that the girls themselves lacked counsel or judgment (*OED, counselless*). Compare the gloss on the line in *TG*, ed. Boffey, p. 35.

202 *yeris of discresioun*. The age of reason (*aetas intelligibilis*) was variously determined to be anywhere between twelve and fifteen years of age in the later Middle Ages.

205 *hir smert*. As their presence in the court of Venus indicates, these female oblates ("many a faire maide," line 207) most lament their enforced celibacy. Pearsall refers somewhat cryptically to the way in which Lydgate is led here "into slightly indecorous irrelevance" (*John Lydgate* [1970], p. 104), but that can only be the case if it is really shameful to acknowledge female sexual desire. The literature of amatory complaint of which *TG* is an example opens up a space in which such desires are expressed, analyzed, and sanctioned.

209–14 *And other next . . . with such treté*. The third group of women to complain concerning a lack of liberty in youth. Their argument for "fredom of eleccioun" in love recalls The Franklin's Tale, *CT* V(F)761–69, and is parodied in other medieval texts (e.g., Jean de Meun's *Romance of the Rose*, lines 13959 ff., and Chaucer's Manciple's Tale, *CT* IX[H]148–54). Also see the explanatory note to lines 342–44.

210   *That.* Here and elsewhere (e.g., lines 216, 639, 1256, 1266, and 1319) the demonstrative has an "instrumental value," conveying the meaning *for the reason that, for that,* or *in that.* On this function of the pronoun, see the discussion in Couormont, "Studies on Lydgate's Syntax," p. 31.

240   *ne durst of hir no.* An example of manifold negation in the poem; see Couormont, "Studies on Lydgate's Syntax," p. 85.

244   *covetise and slouth.* Probably social rather than strictly moral vices, these discourtesies may be conceived along the lines of the "sins" of *CA.* There covetousness (a sub-topic of the fifth book) is a vice of promiscuous and indiscriminate love for more than one lady or a desire for a wealthy lady, and sloth (the main topic of the fourth book) is a vice of absent, unresponsive, or apathetic lovers. Likewise, in *TG* the virtues of the lady (see lines 284–307) are, as we discover, not conventional moral virtues — considering her secret, prohibited desires — but are in the courtly context no less important as signs of her social respectability, good manners, and fine sentiment.

248   *Pallas with hir cristal sheld.* Pallas Athene (Minerva), goddess of war and wisdom, whose shield is a symbol of fortitude in Lydgate's *Troy Book* 2.2557–60. It is not clear whether Pallas and Venus represent allied or opposing forces here (i.e., strength augmenting passion, or virtue opposing beauty). "In this context Pallas probably represents worldly wisdom, since there is also some precedent for associating the goddess with the art of seduction" (Crockett, "Venus Unveiled," p. 77; see *TC* 2.232 and 1062, *CA* 1.1147, and James I's *Kingis Quair,* lines 781ff.). See explanatory note to lines 464 ff.

250–64   *Hou that ther knelid a ladi in my syght . . . in my sighte.* The long string of similes and superlatives, bracketed by repeated reference to the narrator's vision, reemphasizes the subjective, first-person point of view — a voyeuristic male gaze that has been guiding the reader throughout but seems to become especially conspicuous at moments of intensity. Lydgate's narrator is becoming involved as an ardent lover, and his involvement bears comparison with the embarrassed enthusiasms of the narrator in Chaucer's *TC.* The narrator's scrupulous "inspeccioun" (line 278) of the lady will continue for another forty lines with a doting portrait of her physique, courtly manners, and elegant garments — in rhetorical terms, furnishing both an *effictio* (physical attributes) and *ethopoeia* (behavior). Granted, the narrator's comparisons are conventional and formulaic rather than idiosyncratic; compare *BD,* lines 817 ff., and *PF,* lines 298–301, and see Brewer, "Ideal of Feminine Beauty."

253   *Lucifer.* Name of the morning star; also an aspect of Venus (see *TG,* ed. Boffey, p. 88).

271   *brighter than gold were.* The line is cited under the entry for *MED wir* (n.)1b: "fine wire used for filigree or other delicate work; also, metallic thread; a

piece of such thread; also, a wire used in supporting an arrangement of a woman's hair." But it is an eccentric spelling and has as much claim to the subjunctive of the verb "to be."

294   *An exemplarie, and mirrour.* The lady exemplifies or reflects an ideal image of courtly refinement to which others should strive to conform. See also lines 752–54 and 974. On the mirror metaphor in medieval literature, see Grabes, *Mutable Glass*.

299   *al clad in grene and white.* Norton-Smith suggests that green and white signify constancy and chastity. These are the colors of the hawthorn chaplet bestowed by Venus in lines 503–08, where the evergreen appears to signify constancy and youth. The same colors are used in the description of Alceste, a figure of the faithful wife, in *LGW*, F Prol. 242. Crockett, in "Venus Unveiled," p. 78, observes that green is elsewhere a "chaungable colour" (Lydgate's *Fall of Princes* 7.1240), but this does not square with the prior description of the lady (e.g., *hir vertu and hir stabilnes*, line 306). Her colors are black, red, and white in MSS G and S.

303–04   *With sondri rolles on hir garnement / Forto expoune the trouth of hir entent.* "Embroidered texts were a relatively common feature on items of aristocratic dress" (*TG*, ed. Boffey, p. 39). Compare *The Assembly of Ladies*, lines 85–89, 206–08, and 306–08. But equally there may be a faint reminiscence of Boethius' *Consolation of Philosophy* 1.pr1.18–22, describing a vision of Philosophy's robes embroidered with Greek letters (signifying practical and theoretical wisdom). Chaucer's *Boece* was copied in one of the same manuscripts (MS BL Additional 16165) as *TG*, and so may encourage the connection; in fact the lady's "reson" is remarked in line 1053.

310   *De Mieulx en Mieulx.* The lady's motto, "From Better to Better," is a stock phrase in French and Middle English. It is also the motto of the Pastons, a leading family from East Anglia in the fifteenth century, who are known to have owned a copy of *TG* (see *TG*, ed. Schick, p. xxv). There has been an attempt to show that *TG* was composed for a Paston wedding (see MacCracken, "Additional Light"), but it is neither suitable nor very flattering as an epithalamium if there is any suggestion that the lady is escaping an earlier marriage. Moreover, the fact that the lady in the poem bears the motto on her dress before she is betrothed argues against such an occasion. Other attempts to identify the occasion of the work are mentioned in the introduction to this edition. Pearsall, in *John Lydgate* (1970), p. 84, is probably right in observing that the search for a patron and occasion is "something to appease our sense of the preposterousness of a monk writing love-poems."

310-20   The lady's *litel bil* (line 317), which so candidly expresses *the somme of al hir wil* (line 318), attests to her primacy and unusual initiative within the dream vision. As Scanlon observes, "In contrast to the aloof and capricious heroines of romance, this protagonist is from the beginning the source of her own desire rather than a reflection of someone else's. With her entreaty to Venus, it is she who makes the first move. While not unprecedented, this portrayal by

Lydgate is highly unusual. It is not just that he endows this lady with erotic agency. In giving her desire narrative priority, he also gives her the capacity of suffering to the full agonies of the courtly lover, that mark of sublime privilege almost entirely reserved to make figures" ("Lydgate's Poetics," p. 86).

335–69   The lady's complaint is elliptical but suggests the situation of a woman unhappily married or betrothed without her consent (resembling those described in lines 209–14), or possibly subject to a religious vow (like those in lines 196–208). That she is caught in a loveless marriage — and is consequently complaining against neither a prospective marriage nor an undesirable religious vocation — is perhaps suggested by the phrases *bodi knyt* (line 338), *we be on* (line 341), and *undir subjeccion* (line 344), though the lines may simply suggest a reluctance to give up her freedom, specified by the Bible as a consequence of marriage. E.g., Genesis 2:24 or Ephesians 5:22–31: "Let women be subject to their husbands. . . . And they shall be two in one flesh." Only later do we discover that the lady faces a further obstacle in the fact that the object of her affection seems unaware of her love. In effect, Venus has not only to remove the impediment of some prior bond, but she must establish another. It is not Lydgate's style in this poem to divulge the particulars all at once but rather, through carefully controlling the narrative focalization, to release details about the love intrigue little by little. But given the ambiguities of love and affective attachment, some uncertainties may never be resolved.

MSS G and S are equally vague about the situation: in this alternative version of the poem these lines are replaced with others in which the lady complains bitterly about the jealousy of some unidentified figure, perhaps an old husband but possibly a parent or guardian. Following are the stanzas that stand in place of lines 335–69 (based on S):

*335	"So that you list of youre benignyté	
	Goodly to sen and shapen remedye	
	Of wikked tonges and of the creweltee	
	That they may compas thoroghe fals envye	*contrive*
	To quenche theyre venyme and hir felonye	
*340	Wher that they hyndre wymmen giltlesse:	*innocent*
	Styntethe this werre and lat us leven in pees.	
	"I pleyne also upon Jalousye	
	The wylde serpent, the snake tortuous	
	That is so crokid and frownyng on hye	*smugly malcontent*
*345	Ifret with aysel that maketh hem suspecious —	*Consumed; bitterness*
	By al kynde thou art so envyous,	*By nature*
	Of every thing the worste for to deme,	*thinking the worst*
	That ther is nothing that may his hert qweme.	*relieve*
	"Thus is he fryed in his owen grese	*fried; fat*
*350	Torent and torne with his owen rage,	*Ripped*
	And ever froward groynyng causelesse,	*contrary; without reason*
	Whose raysoun fayllethe nowe in olde dotage:	*reason fails*
	This is the maner of croked, fer in age.	*crooked [men], advanced*

Whan they ben coupled with youthe they can no more
*355   But hem waryen — wymmen ben ful sore.   *curse; fully annoyed*

"Thus evere in tourment and yre furyous   *furious anger*
We ben oppressed — allas that harde stounde —   *difficult time*
Ryght as youreself were with Vulcanus
Ageyns youre wille and your hert bounde.
*360   Nowe for the joye whilome that ye founde   *once*
With Mars youre knyght, upon myn compleynt rewe,
For love of yowe that was so fresshe of hewe.

The fear of "wikked tonges" and the dangerous burdens of public exposure remind one of Criseyde's reflections in *TC* 2.729–812 on the unpredictabilities of jealousy and male preoccupation with possession. The Vulcan-Mars analogue does, however, suggest jealous husband rather than simply jealous male.

338   *The bodi knyt, althoughe my thought be fre.* A similar dilemma afflicts a group of female plaintiffs whose bodies are constrained in James I's *Kingis Quair*, lines 631–44.

342–44   *Mi worship sauf, I faile eleccioun . . . undir subjeccion.* The lady is declaring that while she maintains some social respectability in her current situation (e.g., remaining in a loveless situation), it is neither genuinely holy (*of God*) nor natural (*Kynd*). The emphasis on the lady's lack of freedom joins a tissue of intertextual references (see explanatory note to lines 209–14), provoking comparisons with Ami's justification of adultery in Jean de Meun's *Romance of the Rose*, lines 9421 ff.

350–52   Similar sentiments are expressed in Chaucer's *Complaint Unto Pity*, lines 99–100; *PF*, lines 90–91; and in *The Court of Love*, line 988. They all may have origins in Boethius' *Consolation of Philosophy* 3.pr3.33–36. But the lines also recall the moral paradox of Romans 7:14–25: e.g., "For the good which I will, I do not: but the evil which I will not, that I do." If so, the lady's speech is an ironic redefinition of St. Paul's complaint that his innermost spiritual desires ("the law of my mind") are at odds with the body to which he is bound ("the law of sin that is in my members"). This is a bold description of the lady's predicament: is her marriage a sin for which she requires redemption through adultery? Indeed the pathos of the poem relies on what Crockett calls "religious inversion," when, for example, Venus goes on to describe the lady's situation as a "purgatorie" (line 375). On the courtly "religion of love," see Lewis, *Allegory of Love*, pp.18–22, and Spearing, *Medieval Dream-Poetry*, p. 28.

382   *ye.* The first occurrence in the poem of the second person "plural of courtesy," used here by Venus to address the lady. Elsewhere the same decorum is used by the lady towards the knight and the knight towards the lady, thus demonstrating something of their cultivated speech or "daliaunce" (line 291). See Couormont, "Studies on Lydgate's Syntax," pp. 64–66.

385–87   *Withoute chaunge of mutabilité . . . To take louli youre adversité.* The lady's endurance and dedication suggest that she may not be one of those other types of women, represented in antifeminist satire, who are inconstant and indiscriminate. But see Crockett's "Venus Unveiled" for an unsympathetic reading along these lines and the suggestion that the lady is idolatrous, unfaithful, and concupiscent.

389   *old Saturne, my fadur.* "In *Astrol.*, on account of its remoteness and slowness of motion, Saturn was supposed to cause coldness, sluggishness, and gloominess of temperament in those born under its influence, and in general to have a baleful effect on human affairs" (*OED*, *Saturn* 2). Lydgate would have known the story of the birth of Venus from any number of sources, including Jean de Meun's *Romance of the Rose*, lines 5535–54, and, especially, The Knight's Tale, *CT* I(A)2443-78. Saturn can be said to have "fathered" Venus only indirectly when he cast his own father's genitals into the sea, from whence Venus emerged. See also *Fulgentius the Mythographer* 1.1 and 2.1 (trans. Whitbread, pp. 49 and 66–67).

398–404   Following the logic of Pandarus ("By his contrarie is every thyng declared") in *TC* 1.637–48, and expounded elsewhere in Chaucer. This doctrine of contraries has respectable origins in Boethius' *Consolation of Philosophy* 4.pr2.10–12. See also lines 1250–63 in *TG*.

401   *waped and amate.* The *OED* entry for *whaped*, "bewildered, dismayed," cites this very line. *MED wappen* (v.)1c refers to the same collocation as it is employed in Lydgate's *Troy Book* 4.3647, giving it an expansive figurative sense: "to be plunged or driven (into an emotional state), be stricken (with grief), be astonished or dismayed." Potential ambiguity with the word *wappen* (v.)2 "to drape, cover" is admitted. *Amati* is a chess metaphor, i.e., to be "checkmated."

405–11   *Grisilde . . . Penalope . . . Dorigene.* Griselda has been referred to in lines 75–76; Penelope in lines 67–69; see explanatory notes above. Dorigen is the heroine of Chaucer's Franklin's Tale, *CT* V(F)729–1624, where she contemplates suicide to avoid marital infidelity. Oddly, Venus has chosen examples of three faithful wives whose marriages are happily salvaged.

411   *joy is ende and fine of paine.* Sounding like Pandarus again in *TC* 1.952. See Whiting J61.

436   *my brond.* Venus' firebrand as described, for example, in Alan of Lille, *Anticlaudianus* 9.233–34 (trans. Sheridan, p. 210), and invoked in numerous other medieval texts. Compare *PF* 113–14 and The Merchant's Tale (*CT* IV[E]1777); and see *RR*, lines 3705–10. The image figures throughout Lydgate's *Reson and Sensuallyte*, lines 1578–89, 2023–24, 4117–26, 4295, and 6949; and the following epitome appears as a gloss to lines 1578–79 on fol. 223b of MS Fairfax 16: "¶ Hoc fingunt poete propter ardorem libidinis" ("The poets write this because of the flame of desire"). Cupid has his own "brond" at line 838 in *TG*.

447–53   Compare the improving effects of love in *TC* 3.1744–50 and 1786–1806.

453–54   The following stanza is interposed between lines 453 and 454 in the alternative version of the poem that survives in MSS G and S (based on S):

And whi that I so sore to you him bynde
*455   Is that for ye so many have forsake,
Bothe wyse, worthy, and eke gentil of kynde,
Pleynly refused oonly for his sake:
He shal to yow, whether he slepe or wake,
Be evyn suche under hope and drede,
As you list ordeyne of your wommanhed.

454   *this goodli faire, fressh.* Previous editors have placed a comma between *goodli*
            and *faire*, making the latter an adjective and the former an adjectival noun
            as it is later, in line 1402. Precisely this adjective-noun construction, however,
            is used by Lydgate in *Fall of Princes* 1.6930 ("The goodli faire that lith heere
            specheles"); compare also his *Reson and Sensuallyte*, lines 5984-85 ("the goodly
            freshe faire, / That was fairer") and *TG* lines 577 ("The goodli fressh in the
            tempil") and 731 ("That goodli fressh"). Berthelet's print of *TG* clarifies the
            construction by emendation to "goodli ladi," though the alternate version in
            S (the basis for Boffey's edition of *TG*) reads "this goodely, feyre and fresshe."

464 ff.   *Whilom conquered the appel.* Referring to the legend according to which Paris
            was instructed by Jupiter to award a golden apple to the most beautiful of
            three goddesses, Venus, Juno, and Pallas. See, for example, Ovid's *Heroides*
            16.53–88, *Ars Amatoria* 1.245–48 and 1.623–28, and *Remedia Amoris* lines
            709–14. Lydgate would have known that Paris' preference for Venus was
            interpreted by medieval mythographers as a choice of "beauty over wisdom"
            (Crockett, "Venus Unveiled," p. 81; see *Fulgentius the Mythographer*, 2.1 [trans.
            Whitbread, pp. 64–67]). Compare Lydgate's *Troy Book* 2.2635–2792.

492   *subjeccioun.* In courtly love relationships the lady becomes the dominant
            figure exercising control over her male suitor in an inversion of the approved
            power differential of medieval marriage in which the woman is subject to the
            man (e.g., likely alluded to above in line 344). See Duby, *Love and Marriage*,
            p. 62; and Boase, *Origin and Meaning of Courtly Love*.

495–96   The following stanzas are interposed between lines 495 and 496 in the
            alternative version of the poem that survives in MSS G and S (based on S):

And in despyte platly of hem alle	*plainly*
That been to love so contraryous,	
I shal hym cherysshe whatsoevere falle,	*befall*
That is in love so pleyne and vertuous,	
*500 Maugré alle tho that ben desyrous,	*Notwithstanding*
To speken us harme, thoroughe grucching and envye	
Of that ilk serpent cleped Jalousye.	*same; called*
And for hem, lady, if I durst preye,	*dared pray*
Menyng no vengeaunce but correcioun,	
*505 To chastyse hem with torment or they deye	*before; die*
For hir untrowthe and fals suspessyoun,	
That deme the werste in here opynyoun,	*judge the worst*
Withouten desert: wherfore we wowche	*Without justice; affirm*
To punysshe hem for theyre malebouche.	*slander*

*510   To that they may stonden in reproof   *To that [extent]*
        Unto alle loveris for hir cursedenesse,
        Withouten mercy, forsakyn at mescheef,   *in time of distress*
        Whan hem lyste best have mercy of hire distresse,   *they would most desire*
        And for hir falshede and for hir doublenesse,   *duplicity*
*515   And in despyte right as amonge thes foules,   *[Standing] despised; fowls*
        Ben jayis, pyis, thees lapwyngis and thes owlys.   *magpies; lapwings; owls*

503–16   Another version of *TG* (surviving in MSS G and S) deviates at this point.
           Hawthorn branches become roses, and the lady is named (based on S):

        And thanne anon Venus cast adoune
        Into hir lappe roses white and rede
*505   And fresshe of hewe, that wenten envyroun   *all around*
        In compas wyse even aboute hir hede,
        [And bad hyre kepe her of hir goodly hede]
        Whiche shal not fade ne never waxen olde
        If she hir biddyng folowe as she hathe tolde.

*510   And so as ye ben called Margarete,
        Folowethe the feythe that hit dothe specifye:
        This is to seyne, bethe in colde and heete
        Ever of oon hert, as is the dayesye
        Elyche fresshe, whiche that may not dye   *Always fresh*
*515   Thorowe no stormes ne duresse, how it be kene,   *however intense*
        Namore in winter thanne in somer grene.

Norton-Smith, in "Lydgate's Changes," suggests a revision was made to avoid
the negative association of white and red roses with ephemeral pleasures and
passions (compare line 299 of the poem, and see *Troy Book* 2.2531–41); but
note that the same colors have positive connotations elsewhere in Lydgate
(see MacCracken, "Additional Light," p. 135). Margaret may be the given
name of a real lady, as has been supposed by Seaton, *Sir Richard Roos*, p.
375–83. However, it may instead be a sobriquet or an emblematic name, on
which see *TG*, ed. Boffey, p. 51. Bianco, in "New Perspectives," p. 104, suggests that because variation among different versions of the poem concerns
changes in the lady's dress, motto, and chaplet, *TG* was probably "customized"
to fit different occasions and individual ladies. Norton-Smith argues, less per-
suasively, that the changes reflect an artistic process whereby the poem was
revised and improved over time (resulting in the "final" version of the poem
represented, for example, in the present copy-text T).

524   *the goddes shoke hir hede.* As in Chaucer's Knight's Tale, *CT* I(A)2265.

530   *de mieulx en mieulx magré.* Norton-Smith paraphrases the line, "I shall obey
           you better and better in spite of whatever happens" (*TG*, p. 187). The version
           of the poem in MSS G and S has a different motto ("To doon youre biddyng
           humblement magree"), meaning to promise humbly despite it all.

541   *with sparouis and dovues.* Sparrows and doves are the birds most commonly
           affiliated with Venus — sparrows for desire and doves for palpitation, trilling

and cooing, and loyalty. In the General Prologue to *CT*, the Summoner himself is said to be hot and "lecherous as a sparwe" (*CT* I[A]626). See also Chaucer's Summoner's Tale, where the lecherous friar embraces Thomas' wife and "chirketh as a sparwe" (*CT* III[D]1804). For doves and Venus, see *The Romance of the Rose* representations of Venus surmounted by doves (love birds) or being drawn in a chariot powered by doves as in Morgan 132 f. 117v (reprinted in Dunn's edition of *The Romance of the Rose*, p. 336).

546   *I went my wai for the multitude.* One of the emerging parallels between the narrator and the lover, who is first introduced walking alone outside the temple.

553 ff.   *Withoute espiing of eni othir wight.* Except that the lover does not escape the close surveillance of the dreamer-poet who, without any scruples, relates the private spectacle of a man unwittingly falling for an apparently unattainable (possibly married) woman. But the particulars are still vague. The man thinks his only misfortune is to have been wounded by Cupid, and the reader might assume that he loves a different lady: for the narrator holds back (or lacks) crucial bits of information, and the full implications only emerge in the subtle symmetries of language, imagery, and incident. Lydgate's poem consists of a careful choreography of concealment and exposure, the pleasure of which lies partly in the postponing and progressive unveiling of the truth.

567–70   In these lines the lover's lament echoes that of the lady: both speak of being *bound*, lacking *eleccioun*, being put *under subjeccioun*. But the suffering of the man is caused by the affliction of love, whereas for the lady it is being kept from love, whether by social constraint or personal choice.

572 ff.   The man's *sodein aventur* (line 589) is reminiscent of the unexpected conversion of Troilus (who during a visit to a different temple "Wax sodeynly moost subgit unto love," *TC* 1.231), though in Lydgate's poem questions must arise as to why the man has come to Venus' temple in the first place if not already a supplicant.

577   *The goodli fressh in the tempil yonder.* Unable to follow the man's line of sight, we are left to conjecture whether this is the lady from the first part of the poem.

606–09   *A nwe tempest forcasteth now my baarge.* Compare *TC* 1.415–18.

612-13   *lode-ster. . . so hid with cloudes that ben blake.* Literally, the Pole Star, but more figuratively a stable point of reference, the lodestar makes several appearances in Chaucer's work: in The Knight's Tale (*CT* I[A]2056-60), the North Star's legendary origin in the figure of Callisto is among the figures painted on the walls of Diana's temple (see *Metam.* 2.409–509). Troilus twice refers to lodestars in the final book of *TC*: first in reference to Criseyde (5.232) and second in reference to God (5.1392). Lydgate, referring to "cloudes" that hide the star (line 613) seems to mean the literal North Star, with its mythological implications, but the figurative meaning of guidance lost is certainly appropriate for the character of the lover who describes himself as a ship driven by a heedless tempest. These latter images no doubt owe much to Boethius' *Consolation of Philosophy* 1.m7, where "blacke cloudes" obstruct happy navigation

(Chaucer's translation). Compare *Boece* 1.m3 where Boreas blows away the dark clouds to reveal the stars so that, next day, Phebus may shine brightly and "with sodeyn light . . . smyteth with his beemes in merveylyng eien" (Chaucer's translation).

618   *He.* T: *And.* Norton-Smith's emendation. One might justify the manuscript reading on grounds that the loose and awkward syntax is appropriate to the knight's rambling and declamatory complaint in which erratic shifts in subject, tense, and case tend to preponderate. But Norton-Smith's emendation makes the long sentence so much more readable that I have succumbed, in this instance, to the earlier editor's desire for clarity and sound syntax.

629   *knoweth not to whom forto discure.* The lover, filled with torment and pain (line 628) wonders to whom he might disclose his secret love. Compare lines 915-17, when he must meekly *Discure his wound and shew it to his lech* or else die for lack of speech. The passages echo *Boece* 1.p4.4-6, where Lady Philosophy advises the disconsolate Boece: "Yif thou abidest after helpe of thi leche, the byhoveth discovre thy wownde" (Chaucer's translation). Here, the disconsolate lover's *leche* appears to be his lady. He knows that only she can heal him and that can only happen if he "discure his wound and shew it" to her, but how that may be accomplished, either for him or for her, is not readily apparent. So he contines in his *pein.*

641 ff.   *Hope and Drede.* An example of psychomachia (i.e., a battle within the soul between allegorical forces), the medieval taste for which allegories goes back to a well-known fourth-century poem, Prudentius' *Psychomachia.* Compare Troilus and Criseyde on the might of their consummated love, being caught "betwixen drede and sikernesse" (*TC* 3.1315).

689   *But stonde doumb, stil as eni stone.* See Whiting S762.

701   *Citheria.* Another name for Venus.

703–04   *Cirrea . . . thi sete.* Cirrha, an ancient Greek city, is all of a sudden revealed to be the location of the Temple of Glass. Together with Parnassus and Helicon, Cirrha was thought to have been one of the favorite haunts of the Muses. See *TG*, ed. Schick, pp. 104–06.

           The lover's reference to Venus' temple as her *sete* emphasizes that it is not just her home (*MED* n.2c), but that it is also her exalted position of power (*MED* n.1f and g), a symbolism that borders on the sacrilegious.

706   *river of Elicon.* Helicon is a large mountain in Greece.

736–70   These five stanzas apparently drew considerable interest from later medieval anthologizers, who used them variously as stand-alone lyrics. London, BL MS Sloane 1212, for instance, which contains fragments of one of the copies of *TG*, begins with a separate lyric of thirty-six lines, the greater part of which corresponds to lines 736-54 and 762-63 (collected as #139 in Robbins, ed., *Secular Lyrics*). The Bannatyne MS (Edinburgh, National Library of Scotland Adv MS 1.1.6) contains another lyric based on these lines (fol. 220v, see

Boffey and Edwards, *New Index* 851/10), corresponding to lines 743-56 and 764-70.

743   *in myn hert enprentid.* Compare Chaucer's Merchant's Tale, *CT* IV(E)2178.

759   *in vertue nwe and nwe.* Subtly suggestive of the lady's motto.

764   *What wonder than though I be with drede.* He fears rejection because his beloved lady does not betray any expression of "pité" in her demeanor — which is what one should expect of a sophisticated courtly lady, no less than from a married woman. Ironically, if she is the same lady who was the subject of the first part of the poem, then the lover faces greater obstacles than he knows.

778–91   Couormont identifies these lines as containing the "worst passage in our poem," conceding that it nevertheless "does not lack a certain clumsy symmetry." The critic finds fault with what he perceives to be the undue length of the sentence (seventeen lines without a full stop), the proliferation of subordinate clauses, and the deferral of the main clause. See Couormont, "Studies on Lydgate's Syntax," pp. 134–35. But the whole passage is finely balanced and elegantly structured around the two stanzas: each starts off with a comparative statement (*To bene as trwe as* and *To love as wel as*), and the fifth line of each reiterates the vow *Right so shal I.* . . . And there is no lack of verbs throughout the passage, giving it forward momentum and maintaining the focus of the passage on the lover's undying love. See Hardman, "Lydgate's Uneasy Syntax."

778–79   *Antonyus / To Cleopatre.* As recounted in Chaucer's *LGW*, lines 580–705.

780–81   *Or unto Tesbé . . . dethe.* See explanatory note to lines 80–81.

782   *Antropos me sleithe.* Atropos, one of the three Fates, cuts the thread of life. Compare *TC* 4.1546.

785–86   *Achilles . . . Polixene.* See explanatory note to lines 94–95.

787–88   Hercules died when he put on a poisoned tunic given by his wife Deianera (*Dianyre*). The most detailed account of his love of Deianera in Middle English may be found in *CA* 2.2145-2307. Chaucer lists Hercules among the "fals and reccheles" lovers in *HF*, lines 397-404, because he left Deianera for the maiden Ide. Deianera, trying to win his love back, gave him a tunic that she thought had the power to make him love her. Instead, it was poisoned and killed him. The source for both Gower and Chaucer is Ovid's *Heroides* 9. Chaucer relates some of the details in his Monk's Tale, *CT* VII(B²)2095–2142; Gower mentions the pair in *CA* 8.2559–62. Given that Hercules' love for Deianera was so mutable, he makes for a strange exemplary accompaniment to Achilles, and an odd model for the would-be lover to declare to Venus.

815   *stremes of hir eyghen.* Compare *TC* 1.304–05.

829   *For hert, bodi, thought, life, lust, and alle.* Almost verbatim from *TC* 5.1319 (as noted in *TG*, ed. Norton-Smith, p. 189). But see also *BD*, lines 116 and 768.

855–56   *Cupide . . . / He shal ben helping.* Venus appears to be granting the lover's request that the lady be inflamed by Cupid's brand (see lines 836–44), but Venus knows — and yet does not let it slip — that the lady is already desperately in love (see Torti, *Glass of Form*, p. 76). Cupid's blindness is proverbial: see Whiting C634.

866   *trw as eny stele.* Proverbial: see Whiting S709.

905   *For specheles nothing maist thou spede.* Genius' dictum in *CA* 1.1293.

913–17   The analogy goes back to Boethius' *Consolation of Philosophy* 1.pr4.4–6, adapted in the context of Pandarus' advice to Troilus in *TC* 1.857–58. See note to line 169 above. On the proverbial tone of the idea see Whiting L173.

947   *Mi penne I fele quaken as I write.* Compare *TC* 4.13–14. The narrator's involvement reaches a high point in this passage, where it is as if he has some personal stake in the love match. Like the lover in the poem the anguished narrator lacks words to express his "mater" and petitions a goddess to help him. Subtle correspondences suggest that the lover and dreamer are on some level intimately related (see Davidoff, *Beginning Well*, pp. 140–41; Torti, *Glass of Form*, pp. 81–82).

958–59   *Thesiphone / And to hir sustren.* Thesiphone is one of the three Furies, and she is summoned by Chaucer in *TC* 1.6–7 to help him compose "woful vers" and then invoked together with her sisters in 4.22–24 to sustain the tragic ending of the poem.

961–63   *Nou lete youre teris into myn inke reyne . . . to peinte not, but spotte.* The mixture of Furies' tears and ink should so "blot" the paper that the lover's complaint does not appear "painted" (depicted clearly or perhaps artfully) but "spotted" (represented imperfectly, smudging the paper as though with tears) as a proof of sincerity. A version of the "modesty topos," the poet's declaration matches Pandarus' instruction that Troilus write to Criseyde not "scryvenyssh or craftyly" but "Biblotte it with thi teris ek a lite" (*TC* 2.1026–27). Criseyde later receives a letter with "teris al depeynted" in *TC* 5.1599.

970-71   These two lines either reflect or give rise to a popular English song, whose existence is alluded to by Skelton's *Bowge of Court*, line 253, and *Garland of Laurel*, lines 897-904. A fragmentary couplet of a similar (or identical) song, complete with music, can be found in Madrid, Escorial Library MS iv.a.24, fols. 114v-116r (Boffey and Edwards, *New Index*, 2782), printed by Robbins in the notes to the lyric "Parting is Death" (*Secular Lyrics*, p. 275). See Fallows, "Words and Music."

1005   *secré.* Secrecy has especially to be observed in adulterous liaisons, though it is always a courtly virtue: discretion is the soul of elegance. Moreover, secrecy affords lovers a chance for intensifying their pleasure (given the constant threat of exposure). But Bianco, in "New Perspectives," pp. 108–09, is astute in her observation of the paradoxical way in which the secret affair is "played out in a public arena" before a crowd of onlookers and co-celebrants in the Temple of Glass.

1042   *Right as the fressh rodi rose nwe.* Almost verbatim in *PF*, line 442.

1106–1284   The solemn act of binding hearts *in oon* (line 1108), here administered by the goddess and witnessed by her court, finally culminating in a ritual kiss, resembles a marriage ceremony. Kelly, in *Love and Marriage*, thinks it is a clandestine marriage (pp. 291–93). However, it remains doubtful that the lady is free to enter into such a relationship with another man — unless, of course, such a restriction is itself what necessitates a covert coupling. The lovers' quasi-nuptial tying of the knot (see line 1230) may rather be a formalized promise of a future together after the lady's first husband is "disposed of, presumably by death, so that she can marry someone else" (Spearing, *Medieval Dream-Poetry*, p. 176). Lydgate elsewhere uses the image of the knot to signify the marriage bond (e.g., as in *Troy Book* and *Siege of Thebes*), but it can also symbolize a bond of natural affection; see Renoir, "Binding Knot."

               All of this is meant to be some consolation for the other knot binding the lady, but as Torti observes the new knot also reinforces the earlier bond: Venus requires that the lady discharge her prior obligations before consummating her relationship with the new man (*Glass of Form*, pp. 77–78). Venus' ensuing sententious speech, a kind of homily to the lovers, is filled with moral injunctions to be truthful and patient. Venus may not so much represent unregulated sexual desire (as depicted on the walls of the Temple of Glass) as a force for social integration and normative desire. Torti argues that Venus "increasingly speaks in terms of a Christian priest" (p. 80), and some time ago Pearsall called Venus "didactic" and "simply a mouthpiece for advice and instruction" (*John Lydgate* [1970], p. 107). And yet what increases the interest of her moral exhortations is the way they are inevitably inflected by the irony, unorthodoxy, and possible impropriety of the amatory situation. Her reasons for self-restraint are no less pragmatic that those of Pandarus (e.g., *TC* 1.953–61). See Bianco's equally skeptical remarks, in "New Perspectives," pp. 111–14, about the supposed "Christianization" of Venus in *TG*.

1106   *golden cheyne.* The chain of love may be adapted from Boethius' *Consolation of Philosophy* 2.m8. But this is only the last of several references to chains in the poem (compare lines 126–28, 355, 523, and 574), in the earliest of which the notion of binding may not be auspicious: "When she binds the lovers together . . . is she performing a 'marriage' ceremony, or simply echoing the action of Vulcan in the early part of the poem?" (Bianco, "New Perspectives," p. 111).

1120   *my cheyne that maked is of stele.* Venus' steel chain echoes back to line 666, where she promises to make the lady "as trw as eny stele," a statement that is reminiscent of any number of Chaucerian references to love "of steel," love unconditionaly strong and loyal (see, e.g., *HF*, line 683, *TC* 4.325, and *LGW* F.Prol.334). In the alternate version of *TG* in S, however, this line (S1140) is altered to read "my cheyne that is golde yche dele," perhaps under the influence of the "golden cheyne" in line 1106 or of the fact that the arrows of the God of Love are specifically said in *RR* to be all of gold, not steel (lines 946–47).

1122   *his long servise*. As if conforming to the unities of time and place, the temporal sequence of allegorical events represents a condensed and anachronistic version of real events. Supposedly a "long" time has passed since the lover was first smitten.

1128   *chaunge for no nwe*. Compare *LGW*, line 1235.

1138–39   *Late him for trouth then finde trouth agein*. Compare *TC* 2.390–92.

1143   *And love for love woulde wele biseme*. See Whiting L506.

1153   *constant as a walle*. See Whiting W11–18. The line is reminiscent of Chaucer's Clerk's Tale (*CT* IV[E]1047), particularly in light of earlier references to Griselda in lines 75–76 and 405 of *TG*. See Scanlon, "Lydgate's Poetics," pp. 90–91.

1157   *Tempest thee not but ever in stidfastnes*. Compare Chaucer's "Truth: Balade de Bon Conseyl," line 8: "Tempest thee noght . . ."

1164   *champartie*. "The practice of aiding a litigant for a share of the matter in dispute, champerty," or "to hold one's own (orig., keep or get one's share), contend successfully" (*MED* 1 and 2a.).

1183   *Woorde is but winde*. A proverb found, among other places, in *CA* 3.2768. See Whiting W643.

1193   *So thee to preve, thou ert put in delay*. The principle seems to be intrinsic to Lydgate's poem, structured as it is around seductive deferrals and displacements, frustrating the reader's desire for disclosure. The payoff is greater pleasure, as Venus would say: "folk also rejosshe more of light / That thei with derknes were waped and amate" (lines 400–01; compare lines 1250–63). Lydgate seems to be complicit with Venus.

1225   *my key of gold*. Compare Guillame de Lorris, *Romance of the Rose*, lines 1999–2004.

1232–33   *Saturne and Jove and Mars . . . And eke Cupide*. Bianco, in "New Perspectives," pp. 112–13, says these gods are "a most unpromising collection" given their appearances earlier in the poem. Saturn has been the cause of the lady's misfortune (lines 388–89); Jove humiliated himself for one woman (lines 117–20), changing shape again to seduce another (lines 121–25); Mars was caught in flagrante delicto with the adulterous Venus (lines 126–28); and of course Cupid is blind and notoriously cruel and capricious (e.g., line 114). It is always the case that the unsavory and sexually promiscuous behavior of the gods is a liability, but perhaps they are meant here only as benign influences. In *TC* 3.625, it is the teaming up of Saturn and Jove that produces the great rainstorm that, for better or for worse, helps bring Troilus and Criseyde together while Troilus worries about the bad aspects of Mars and Saturn at his birth (*TC* 3.715–19), which he asks Venus to avert, through her supplication of Jove, "Thy fader." As we have already seen in relation to Venus, for Lydgate ancient mythology is adaptable, multivalent, and employed for limited and local effects.

1303   *Caliopé / And al hir sustren.* Muse of epic poetry; together with her sisters she sings hymns of praise in *HF*, lines 1399–1401, and she is invoked to help the poet communicate the joy of the lovers in *TC* 3.45–48.

1308–09   *Orpheus . . . with his harp.* . . . Orpheus is the legendary musician who features in Boethius' *Consolation of Philosophy* 3.m12 and the Middle English romance *Sir Orfeo* (c. 1300). Derived from classical sources, e.g., *Metam.* 10.1–85. See also *Fulgentius the Mythographer,* 3.10 (trans. Whitbread, pp. 96–98).

1310–11   *Amphioun.* King Amphioun, who builds the walls of Thebes with the power of his harp song (or "eloquence"), as Lydgate relates in *Siege of Thebes,* lines 201 ff. Mentioned, for example, in Chaucer's Merchant's Tale, *CT* IV(E)1716, and Manciple's Tale, *CT* IX(H)116–17, and found variously in Statius, Ovid, Horace, and Boccaccio.

1341–61   This song, sung in praise of Venus by the lovers in the temple, takes the form of a three-stanza ballade including a refrain.

1348   *Esperus.* The evening star and another name for Venus (*TG,* ed. Boffey, p. 88).

1365   *Oute of my slepe anone I did awake.* Chaucer's dreamer is similarly awakened by a roundel sung at the end of *PF,* lines 680–95.

1379 ff.   *I purpose here to maken and to write / A litil tretis.* Like Chaucer at the end of *TC* 5.1765–78, Lydgate vows he will compose a poem (*litil tretis*) in praise of women. The *simpil tretis* subsequently referred to in line 1387 may refer to the future encomium or to the present dream vision, but in any case the gesture towards writing is comparable to *BD,* lines 1330–34. Davidoff, in *Beginning Well,* pp. 144–45, argues that the resolve to write shows that the dreamer-poet has discovered in his dream the solution to his troubles: "For specheles nothing maist thou spede" (line 905). Early manuscripts attach to the poem a 628-line *Compleynt,* the circumstances of which are not relevant to the dream but which appears to have been treated by scribes (Pearsall postulates a "literal-minded scribe," *John Lydgate* [1970], p. 109) as a continuation of Lydgate's *TG.*

1389–90   *Forto expoune . . . the significaunce.* The poet thinks his dream is worth interpreting (technically speaking, it is a *somnium* rather than a mundane *insomnium*). On the different types of dream see Chaucer's discussion at the beginning of the *HF,* lines 1–52, the typology of which is originally derived from Macrobius' *Somnium Scipionis* 1.3 (*Commentary on the Dream of Scipio,* trans. Stahl, pp. 87–89).

1392   *my ladi may it loke.* The identity of the lady throughout the closing section of the poem has been the cause of great uncertainty. She can be taken to be the "real life" counterpart of the lady envisaged within the dream vision. If so, then there are grounds for thinking of the dream as an objectification and elaboration of the distress that kept the poet awake at the beginning. The man within the dream would be no less than a projection of the dreamer-poet — demonstrating the truth of Chaucer's notion that dreams are wish-fulfilment fantasies in which a lover will imagine winning his lady (*PF,* line 105; the notion was originally derived from Macrobius' *Somnium Scipionis* 1.3.3

[*Commentary on the Dream of Scipio*, trans. Stahl, pp. 88–89]). On the conventional "need-to-fulfilment" structure of dream visions in general and of *TG* in particular, see Davidoff, *Beginning Well*, pp. 60–80 and 135–46. On the other hand, the dream may have provoked the dreamer's love for some lady he knows or has yet to identify; or he may be referring first of all to Venus and then to some female patron for whom he writes. All of this is part of the framing fiction of *TG*, carefully contrived by the monk Lydgate (not a courtly lover himself), to leave open more than one possibility for interpretation. As the previous lines implied, the meaning of the dream is not self-evident and requires interpretation.

1393 ff.   *Nou go thi wai, thou litel rude boke.* Imitating the envoy to *TC* 5.1786 ff. See also Gower's *Vade liber purus*, with which he concludes *CA*.

1399   The alternative version of the poem contained in MSS G and S stops here, and so does not include the envoy or dedication found in MS Tanner.

 TEXTUAL NOTES

ABBREVIATIONS: **F** = Oxford, Bodleian Library, MS Fairfax 16; **B** = Oxford, Bodleian Library, MS Bodley 638; **G** = Cambridge, University Library, MS Gg. 4.27; **MED** = *Middle English Dictionary*; **S** = London, British Library, MS Additional 16165; **T** = Oxford, Bodleian Library, MS Tanner 346 [base-text]; **NS** = *John Lydgate: Poems*, ed. Norton-Smith; **Sch** = *Temple of Glas*, ed. Schick.

Title	*The Temple of Glas.* The title is so ascribed in T, as well as all other MSS except F and B; see Sch, p. xvii.
2	*For.* T: *ffor.* Transcribed as a capital letter throughout this edition.
12	*longe.* T. *long.* Final *-e* has been added in several instances throughout for the sake of meter (i.e., eurhythmy). Besides *longe* (lines 12, 1373) changes of this nature include *thoughte* (15, 532); *reporte* (43); *moste* (61, 186); *myghte* (68, 89, 137, 285, 286, 309, 595, 1021); *fresshe* (70, 93, 184); *trwe* (71); *herte* (80, 312, 337, 363, 726, 756, 825, 839, 920, 921, 945, 986, 1182, 1205); *dide* (80, 116, 945, 1055, 1233); *thilke* (81); *Troie* (95); *yunge, yonge* (106, 193, 780); *ofte* (169, 193, 231, 669); *kynde* (224); *finde* (242, 1138); *beste* (292); *harde* (361, 957); *shulde* (191, 372); *rejosshe* (400); *woulde* (591, 893, 1143); *hurte* (601, 813); *stonde* (689); *thanke* (774); *peyne* (798); *graunte* (804); *brente* (840); *waie* (897); *roughte* (939); *helpe* (952, 959); *peinte* (963); *righte* (975); *grete* (984); *bothe* (1108); *joye* (1129); *weie* (1140); *olde* (1222); *ferse* (1236); *founde* (1239); *withoute* (1254); *mente* (1288); *telle* (1289); *juste* (1331); *whiche* (1334).
13	*atte.* T *at.* So Sch and NS.
16	*a.* T omits. So Sch and NS.
17	*wildirnesse.* T: *wildirnes.* Supported by F and B.
18	*liklynesse.* T: *liknesse.* So Sch and NS.
30	*atte.* T *at.* So Sch and NS.
32	*Tofor.* T: *To fore.* Joined throughout.
33	*within and withoute.* T: *with in and with oute.* Joined throughout.
55	*Cartage.* T: *Carge.* So Sch and NS.
72	*she.* T: *sho.* So NS.
74	*daiesie.* T: *daisie.* So Sch and NS.
75	*also.* T omits. So Sch and NS and supported by F and B.
84	*forwrynkled.* T: *forwrynkked.* So NS.
88	*for his trespas.* T omits *for.* So Sch and NS; but NS misreads *trepas.*

96–97	*walkynge up and doun.* / *Ther sawe I.* T omits two half-lines at this point, with a large ascending decorative initial causing a break in the text and the rhyme scheme. T reads *Al this sawe I writen eke the hole tale.* Emended following the other MSS; so Sch and NS.
112	*an arow.* T: *anoro.* So Sch and NS.
113	*thurughoute.* T: *thurugh oute.*
115	*Daphne.* T: *Diane.* So Sch; NS emends to *Dane.*
116	*that.* T omits. So NS.
119	*a.* T omits. So Sch and NS.
123	*passing.* T: *passig.* So Sch and NS.
	of. T: *was.* So Sch and NS.
129	*poesie.* T: *poesre.* So Sch and NS.
130	*Philologye.* T: *Philloge.* So Sch and NS.
133	*lowli did.* T: *did lowli.* So Sch and NS and supported by F and B.
149	*obak.* T: *o bak.* So NS.
150	*causeles.* T: *causles.* So Sch and NS.
154	T omits line. Sch and NS derive the missing line from other MSS.
160	*on.* Sch and NS emend to *in*; see *MED on* 20.d.
171	*a.* T omits. So Sch and NS.
175	*on.* T: *in.* NS emends to *on*, Sch to *of.*
192	*soote.* T: *sute.* Sch emends to *So soote.*
199	*That conseiles.* Sch emends conjecturally to *That were constrayned.*
208	*That.* T: *Than.* So Sch and NS.
213	*at.* T omits. So Sch and NS.
216	T omits line. Missing line derived from the other MSS; so Sch and NS.
227	*geve.* T: *yeve.*
249	*statue.* T: *statute.* So Sch.
262	*hir.* T: *hirħ.*
281	*geven.* T: *yeven.*
287	*or.* T: *er.* So Sch and NS.
309–10	S, an early version of the poem, gives an alternative reading in these lines; see explanatory notes. In T the lady's motto is rubricated here and in line 530.
311	*This to.* Sch emends to *This is to.*
320	T omits line. Missing line derived from the other MSS; so Sch and NS.
322	*world.* T: *word.* So Sch and NS.
323	*hauteyn ben.* T: *ha doten.* So Sch and NS and supported by F and B.
325	*releser.* T: *relese.* Emended on strength of B and other MSS.
327	*Thurugh.* T: *Thurught.* So Sch and NS.
335–69	Lines replaced by four stanzas in S; see explanatory notes to lines 321-69.
345	*ar.* T: *er.* So Sch and NS.
365	*albeit.* T: *al be it.*
377	*sadde.* T: *sad.* So Sch and NS.
405	*Grisilde was assaied atte.* T: *Grisild was assaied at.* Accepting the metrical improvement of Sch and NS on authority of F.
408	*her.* T omits. So Sch and NS.
411	*Thus ever joy is ende.* T has been changed to read: *Thus evere joy is ended.*
420	*wounde.* T: *woude.* So Sch and NS.

427	*possession*. T: *possion*. So Sch and NS.
449	*benygne face*. T has what appears to be *grace* (in an abbreviated form matching the spelling of the word found, for example, in lines 475 and 490) between *benygne* and *face*. Neither Sch nor NS register the extraneous word.
453–54	Other versions of the poem interpolate another stanza; see explanatory notes.
456	*had*. T: *hath*. So Sch and NS.
463	*beaute*. T omits. So Sch and NS.
465	*his hygh request*. T omits. So Sch and NS and supported by F and B.
478	*Sith ye, my ladi, list nou to appese*. T: *With the, my ladi, list nou to have peas*. Following Sch and NS on authority of F and B, but changing to *ye* instead of *thee*.
486	*brought*. T: *brough*. So Sch and NS.
489	*hert*. T: *hort*. So NS.
491	*humbeli*. T: *humbli*. So Sch and NS.
494–95	With the support of F and B, Sch and NS emend these lines to read: *Unto his last: now laude and reverence / Be to youre name and to your excellence.*
495–96	Other versions of the poem interpolate another three stanzas; see explanatory notes.
504–06	Other versions of the poem read: *roses white and rede / So fressh of hewe.* See explanatory notes.
505	*hawethorn*. T: *hawthorun*. So Sch and NS.
518	*for*. T omits. So Sch and NS.
530	S and G have a different motto; see explanatory notes.
530a–b	*Explicit prima pars / Icy commence le secund parti de la songe.* So T, NS. F, B, G, S, Sch omit.
541	*And*. T: *An*. So Sch and NS.
554	*if*. Blotted out in T.
563	*in*. Sch emends to *by*.
565	*by himself*. T: *bym self*. So Sch and NS.
587	*him*. Sch and NS emend to *hir*. I retain the masculine pronoun since it can refer back to God (579) or even the God of Love (572) under whose subjection the knight suffers for the lady.
602	*take*. T: *tast*. So NS.
608	*possid*. T: *passid*. So Sch and NS and supported by F and B.
612	Sch emends to *I ne may not se*; NS to *(I wot) I mai not se*. But the original can stand as a sensible and recognizable type of the "Lydgatian" line.
618	*He*. T: *And*. So NS.
635	*myn owne*. T: *my*. So Sch and NS.
638	*That am distraught within myselfen so*. MS: *That I am distraught within myself so*. So Sch and NS.
639	*forto*. T: *for*. So Sch and NS.
645	*iset*. Sch emends to *set*.
655	Sch and NS emend *hold* (i.e., detained, urged, obliged) to *bold*, despite evidence of other MSS.
657	*contrarie*. T: *contrare*. So NS.
664	*myschef*. Sch and NS emend to *myself*.
666	*she*. T: *sho*. So NS.

673   *thorugh*. T: *though*. So Sch and NS.
676   *therewithal bitt*. T: *therewith bitter*. So Sch and NS.
677   Sch emends to *be bold* but nevertheless retains the sense of the original in his
        gloss ("Hope makes me look for mercy"), appropriately given the next
        line about the face of the beloved.
694   *thoughte*. T: *though*. So Sch and NS.
703   *al*. T omits. So Sch and NS.
705   *oft*. T: *of*. So Sch and NS.
706   *Elicon*. T: *eleccion*. So Sch and NS.
711   *Benigneli*. T: *Benigli*. So Sch and NS.
719   *so dere*. T: *sodere*.
726   *fire hire*. T: *hire fire*. So Sch and NS.
736   *geve*. T: *yeve*.
        hardines. NS misreads *herdines*.
741   *woid*. Sch and NS emend to *vowed*, but the spelling also occurs in 1128.
747   *kyndenes*. T: *kyndnes*. So Sch and NS.
767   *therfor*. T: *therfro*. So Sch and (silently) NS.
771   *avowe*. T: *avove*. So Sch and (silently) NS.
773   *humbeli*. T: *humble*. So NS.
785   *as wel*. T: *aswel*.
802   *enclyne*. NS misreads *enclynce*.
808   *your*. T omits. Sch and NS make the addition on the authority of other MSS.
821   Second *I*. T omits. So Sch and NS with support from F and B.
843   *flaumed*. T: *baumed*. So Sch and NS with support from F and B.
849   *benygneli*. T: *benygli*. So Sch and NS.
851   *goodeli*. T: *goodli*. So Sch and NS.
852   *humbelie*. T: *humblie*. So Sch and NS.
872   *Demen*. T: *Semen*. So Sch and NS.
877   *dilacioun*. T: *dillusioun*. So Sch and NS with support from F and B.
885   *enspiren*. T: *enspire*. So Sch and NS.
901   *sage*. T: *sange*.
915   *hurtis*. Sch emends to *hertis*.
928   NS adds *may* apparently to avoid a "Lydgatian" line.
939   *that*. Sch emends to *though*.
961   *myn inke*. T: *myn eighe inke*. "Eighe" is marked for deletion.
967   *hidde*. T: *hid*. So Sch and NS.
980   *helpen*. T: *help*. So Sch and NS.
983   *to*. T omits. So Sch and NS.
988   *hidde*. T: *hid*. So Sch and NS.
990   *hath bound me to*. T: *me hath bound unto*. So Sch and NS.
997   *Whereso*. T: *Wheresoever*. So Sch and NS and supported by F and B.
1000   *goodeli*. T: *goodl*. So NS. Sch emends to *goodli*.
1008   *yow allone*. T: *yow ben allone*. So Sch and NS following F and B.
1009   *gan*. T: *began*. So Sch and NS following F and B.
1012   *deien*. T: *dein*. So Sch and NS.
1013   *any*. T: *anay*. Second "a" marked for deletion.
1020   *womanli*. T: *womanl*. So Sch and NS.

1023	*for.* T omits. So Sch and NS.
1029	*my wittes.* T: *as my wittes.* So Sch and NS.
1034	*atte.* T: *at.* So NS.
1045	*femynynité.* T: *femynyte.* So Sch and NS.
1047	*humbele.* T: *humble.* So Sch. NS emends to *humblei.*
1057	*behest.* T: *hest.* So Sch and NS.
1082	*list.* T omits. So Sch and NS.
1087	*hidde.* T: *hid.* So Sch and NS.
1088	*hertes.* T: *hert.* So Sch. NS emends to *hertis.*
1098	*relesen.* T: *plesen.* So Sch and NS.
1105	*mekeli.* T: *mekel.* So Sch and NS.
1110	*benygne.* NS misreads *benyngne.*
1113	*as hit is.* T: *at his.* So Sch and NS.
1138	*trouth₂.* T omits. So Sch and NS.
1144	*geve.* T: *yeve.*
1161	*do them.* Sch emends to *hem don.*
1165	*alle.* T: *al.* So Sch and NS.
1188	*herte myne.* T: *hertes mynd.* So Sch and NS following F and B.
1189	*hir yyve.* Sch emends to *yyve hir.*
1190	*othir.* T: *oth.* So Sch and NS.
1191	Sch and NS remove *that,* though the dactyl seems acceptable.
1208	*worldis.* T: *wordis.* So Sch and NS.
1217	*Whan.* T: *Wan.* So Sch and NS.
1229	*bonde.* T: *bounde.* So Sch and NS with support from F and B.
1230	*is.* T: *ye.* So Sch and NS.
1234	*overmore.* Sch and NS emend to *evermore;* but see *MED overmor(e).*
1237	*falle.* T: *fal.* So Sch and NS.
1257	*in.* T omits. So Sch and NS.
1270	*knot.* T: *þnot.* Þ marked for erasure. So Sch and NS.
1273	*wele.* Sch emends to *well,* NS to *wel.* Final *–e* was in the process of losing phonetic value during this period, but full feminine rhyme remains a possibility.
1278	*so forthwith in.* T: *soforthe within.* So Sch and NS.
1280	*toke.* T: *eke.* So Sch and NS.
1282	*fulfillyng.* T: *fufillyng.* So Sch and NS.
1283	*wise.* T: *vise.* So Sch and NS.
1284	*As.* T: *And.* So Sch and NS.
1289	*thogh.* T: *thow.*
1290	*that.* T and Sch omit. So NS.
1291	*For.* T: *Forthe.* So Sch and NS.
1293	*of.* T: *to.* So Sch and NS with support from F and B.
1297	*shal.* T omits. So Sch and NS with support from F and B.
1302	*Geve.* T: *yeve.*
1305	*Sone.* Sch enends to *Gunne.* NS emends to *Gan.*
1318	*Withouten.* T: *Withoute.* So Sch and NS.
1328	*presscience.* T: *presence.* A majority of MSS read *presence* yielding a four-beat line, and in order to correct for the deficient meter here and three lines

later in the same stanza I follow previous editors by emending on the basis of S.

1331   *providence*. T: *prudence*. So Sch and NS.

1333   *contune*. T: *tyme*. So Sch and NS.

1336   *gone*. Sch and NS emend to *gonne*.

1346   *Be*. T: *We*. So Sch and NS.

1349   *sterre*. Sch and NS emend to *stere*.

1363   *Which*. T: *With*. So Sch and NS.

1377   *Sein*. T: *Sei*. So Sch and NS.

1383   *fulle*. T: *ful*. So Sch and NS.

1384   *bounteous*. T: *bounteuos*. Sch emends to *bounteuous*.

 **BIBLIOGRAPHY**

Alan of Lille. *Anticlaudianus, or The Good and Perfect Man.* Trans. James J. Sheridan. Toronto: Pontifical Institute of Medieval Studies, 1973.

The Assembly of Ladies. See *The Floure and the Leafe.*

Augustine. *Concerning the City of God against the Pagans.* Trans. Henry Bettenson. New York: Penguin, 1972.

The Bannatyne Manuscript: National Library of Scotland, Advocates' MS. 1.1.6. Intro. Denton Fox and William A. Ringler. London: Scolar Press in association with the National Library of Scotland, 1980.

Barthes, Roland. *The Pleasure of the Text.* Trans. Richard Miller. New York: Hill and Wang, 1975.

Bianco, Susan. "A Black Monk in the Rose Garden: Lydgate and the *Dit Amoureux* Tradition." *Chaucer Review* 34 (1999), 60–68.

———. "New Perspectives on Lydgate's Courtly Verse." In Cooney, pp. 95–115.

Boase, Roger. *The Origin and Meaning of Courtly Love: A Critical Study of European Scholarship.* Manchester: Manchester University Press, 1977.

Bodleian Library MS Fairfax 16. Intro. John Norton-Smith. London: Scolar Press, 1979.

Boethius. *The Consolation of Philosophy.* In *Boethius.* Ed. and trans. H. F. Stewart, E. K. Rand, and S. J. Tester. Loeb Classical Library 74. Cambridge, MA: Harvard University Press, 1973.

Boffey, Julia. "English Dream Poems of the Fifteenth Century and Their French Connections." In *Literary Aspects of Courtly Culture: Selected Papers from the Seventh Triennial Congress of the International Courtly Literature Society.* Ed. Donald Maddox and Sara Sturm-Maddox. Cambridge: D. S. Brewer, 1994. Pp. 113–21.

———. "'Forto compleyne she had gret desire': The Grievances Expressed in Two Fifteenth-Century Dream-Visions." In Cooney, pp. 116–28.

———. *Fifteenth-Century English Dream Visions.* See Lydgate, *The Temple of Glas.*

Boffey, Julia, and A. S. G. Edwards. *A New Index of Middle English Verse.* London: The British Library, 2005.

Brewer, D. S. "The Ideal of Feminine Beauty in Medieval Literature, Especially 'Harley Lyrics,' Chaucer, and Some Elizabethans." *Modern Language Review* 50 (1955), 257–69.

Bronfman, Judith. *Chaucer's Clerk's Tale: The Griselda Story Received, Rewritten, Illustrated.* Garland Studies in Medieval Literature. New York: Garland Publishing, 1994.

Brown, Peter, ed. *Reading Dreams: The Interpretation of Dreams from Chaucer to Shakespeare.* Oxford: Oxford University Press, 1999.

Chaucer, Geoffrey. *The Riverside Chaucer.* Gen. ed. Larry D. Benson. Third ed. Boston: Houghton Mifflin Company, 1987.

Connolly, Margaret. *John Shirley: Book Production and the Noble Household in Fifteenth-Century England.* Aldershot: Ashgate, 1998.

Cooney, Helen, ed. *Nation, Court and Culture: New Essays on Fifteenth-Century English Poetry.* Dublin: Four Courts Press, 2001.

Couormont, André. "Studies on Lydgate's Syntax in *The Temple of Glas.*" *Bibliothèque de la Faculté des Lettres de l'Université de Paris* 28 (1912), 1–144.

Crockett, Bryan. "Venus Unveiled: Lydgate's *Temple of Glas* and the Religion of Love." In *New Readings of Late Medieval Love Poems*. Ed. David Chamberlain. Lanham, MD: University Press of America, 1993. Pp. 67–93.

Culler, Jonathan. *The Pursuit of Signs: Semiotics, Literature, Deconstruction*. Ithaca, NY: Cornell University Press, 1981.

Davidoff, Judith M. *Beginning Well: Framing Fictions in Late Middle English Poetry*. London: Associated University Presses, 1988.

Davis, Norman, ed. *Paston Letters and Papers of the Fifteenth Century*. 2 vols. Oxford: Clarendon Press, 1971–72.

de Jong, Mayke. *In Samuel's Image: Child Oblation in the Early Medieval West*. Leiden: E. J. Brill, 1996.

Duby, Georges. *Love and Marriage in the Middle Ages*. Trans. Jane Dunnett. Chicago: University of Chicago Press, 1994.

Duffell, Martin J. "Lydgate's Metrical Inventiveness and His Debt to Chaucer." *Parergon* n.s. 18.1 (2000), 227–49.

Dunbar, William. *The Complete Works*. Ed. John Conlee. Kalamazoo, MI: Medieval Institute Publications, 2004.

Ebin, Lois A. *John Lydgate*. Boston: Twayne, 1985.

———. *Illuminator, Makar, Vates: Visions of Poetry in the Fifteenth Century*. Lincoln: University of Nebraska Press, 1988.

Edwards, A. S. G. "Lydgate Manuscripts: Some Directions for Future Research." In *Manuscripts and Readers in Fifteenth-Century England: Essays from the 1981 Conference at the University of York*. Ed. Derek Pearsall. Cambridge: D. S. Brewer, 1983. Pp. 15–26.

———. "Lydgate Scholarship: Progress and Prospects." In *Fifteenth-Century Studies*. Ed. R. F. Yeager. Hamden, CT: Archon Books, 1984. Pp. 29–47.

Eisner, Sigmund. *The Tristan Legend: A Study in Sources*. Evanston, IL: Northwestern University Press, 1969.

Fallows, D. "Words and Music in Two English Songs of the Mid-Fifteenth Century." *Early Music* 5 (1977), 38-43.

The Floure and the Leafe, The Assembly of Ladies, The Isle of Ladies. Ed. Derek Pearsall. Kalamazoo, MI: Medieval Institute Publications, 1990.

Fulgentius. *Fulgentius the Mythographer*. Trans. Leslie George Whitbread. Columbus: Ohio State University Press, 1971.

Gower, John. *The English Works of John Gower*. Ed. G. C. Macaulay. 2 vols. EETS e.s. 81–82. London: Paul Trench, Trübner, and Co., 1900–01; rpt. London: Oxford University Press, 1957.

———. *Confessio Amantis*. Ed. Russell A. Peck. 3 vols. Kalamazoo, MI: Medieval Institute Publications, 2000–06. [Vol. 1: Prologue, Books 1 and 8; vol. 2: Books 2–4; vol. 3: Books 5–7.]

Grabes, Herbert. *The Mutable Glass: Mirror-Imagery in Titles and Texts of the Middle Ages and English Renaissance*. Trans. Gordon Collier. Cambridge: Cambridge University Press, 1982.

Griffiths, R. A. *The Reign of King Henry VI*. Second ed. Gloucestershire: Sutton, 1998.

Guillaume de Lorris and Jean de Meun. *The Romance of the Rose*. Trans. Charles Dahlberg. Hanover, NH: University Press of New England, 1986.

———. *The Romance of the Rose*. Trans. Harry W. Robbins. Ed. Charles W. Dunn. New York: E. P. Dutton, 1962.

Hardman, Phillipa. "Lydgate's Uneasy Syntax." In Scanlon and Simpson, pp. 12-35.

Iser, Wolfgang. *The Act of Reading: A Theory of Aesthetic Response*. Baltimore: The Johns Hopkins University Press, 1978.

James I. *The Kingis Quair*. In *The Kingis Quair and Other Prison Poems*. Ed. Linne R. Mooney and Mary-Jo Arn. Kalamazoo, MI: Medieval Institute Publications, 2005. Pp. 17–112.

Jones, Michael. "Catherine (1401–1437)." *Oxford Dictionary of National Biography*. Oxford: Oxford University Press, 2004.

Kelly, Henry Ansgar. *Love and Marriage in the Age of Chaucer*. Ithaca, NY: Cornell University Press, 1975.

Kruger, Steven F. *Dreaming in the Middle Ages*. Cambridge: Cambridge University Press, 1992.

Lawton, David. "Dullness and the Fifteenth Century." *ELH* 54.4 (Winter 1987), 761–99.

Lerer, Seth. *Chaucer and His Readers: Imagining the Author in Late-Medieval England*. Princeton, NJ: Princeton University Press, 1993.

Lewis, C. S. *The Allegory of Love: A Study in Medieval Tradition*. Oxford: Clarendon Press, 1936.

Livy. *Livy*. Trans. B. O. Foster. 14 vols. Vol. 1: *History of Rome*, Books I and II. Loeb Classical Library. Cambridge, MA: Harvard University Press, 1919.

Lydgate, John. *A Complaynt of a Loveres Lyfe*. In *John Lydgate: Poems*. Ed. John Norton-Smith. Oxford: Clarendon Press, 1966. Pp. 47–66 and 160–76.

———. *The Fall of Princes*. Ed. Henry Bergen. 4 vols. Washington, DC: The Carnegie Institution of Washington, 1923–27.

———. *The Minor Poems of John Lydgate*. Ed. Henry Noble MacCracken. 2 vols. EETS e.s. 107, o.s. 192. London: Oxford University Press, 1911–34. Rpt. 1961–62.

———. *Reson and Sensuallyte*. Ed. Ernst Sieper. 2 vols. EETS e.s. 84 and 89. Bungay: Richard Clay & Sons, 1901–03; rpt. London: Oxford University Press, 1965.

———. *The Serpent of Division*. Ed. Henry Noble MacCracken. London: Oxford University Press, 1911.

———. *The Siege of Thebes*. Ed. Robert R. Edwards. Kalamazoo, MI: Medieval Institute Publications, 2001.

———. *The Temple of Glas*. In *Lydgate's Temple of Glas*. Ed. J. Schick. EETS e.s. 60. London: Kegan Paul, Trench, Trübner & Co., 1891. [Based on MS Tanner 346.]

———. *The Temple of Glas*. In *John Lydgate: Poems*. Ed. John Norton-Smith. Clarendon Medieval and Tudor Series. Oxford: Clarendon Press, 1966. Pp. 67–112, 176–91. [Based on MS Tanner 346.]

———. *The Temple of Glas*. In *Fifteenth-Century English Dream Visions: An Anthology*. Ed. Julia Boffey. Oxford: Oxford University Press, 2003. Pp. 15–89. [Based on MS Additional 16165.]

———. *Troy Book*. In *Lydgate's Troy Book, A. D. 1412–20*. Ed. Henry Bergen. 4 vols. EETS e.s. 97, 103, 106, and 126. London: Kegan Paul, Trench, Trübner and Co., 1906–35. Rpt. as 2 vols. Millwood, NY: Kraus Reprint Co., 1973.

Lynch, K. L. *The High Medieval Dream Vision*. Stanford, CA: Stanford University Press, 1988.

MacCracken, Henry Noble. "Additional Light on the *Temple of Glas*." *PMLA* 23 (1908), 128–40.

Macrobius. *Commentary on the Dream of Scipio*. Trans. William Harris Stahl. New York: Columbia University Press, 1952.

Manuscript Bodley 638: A Facsimile. Intro. Pamela Robinson. Facsimile Series of the Works of Geoffrey Chaucer 2. Norman, OK: Pilgrim Books, 1982.

Manuscript Pepys 2006: A Facsimile. Intro. A. S. G. Edwards. Facsimile Series of the Works of Geoffrey Chaucer 6. Norman, OK: Pilgrim Books, 1985.

Manuscript Tanner 346: A Facsimile. Intro. Pamela Robinson. Facsimile Series of the Works of Geoffrey Chaucer 1. Norman, OK: Pilgrim Books, 1980.

Manzalaoui, Mahmoud A. "Lydgate and English Prosody." In *Cairo Studies in English*. Ed. M. Wahba. Cairo: Costa Tsoumas, 1960. Pp. 87–104.

Martianus Capella. *Martianus Capella and the Seven Liberal Arts*. Vol. 2: *The Marriage of Philology and Mercury*. Trans. William Harris Stahl and Richard Johnson, with E. L. Burge. New York: Columbia University Press, 1977.

Miskimin, Alice. "Patterns in *The Kingis Quair* and the *Temple of Glas*." *Papers on Language and Literature* 13 (1977), 339–61.

Moore, Samuel. "Patrons of Letters in Norfolk and Suffolk c. 1450." *PMLA* 27 (1912), 188–207.

Norton-Smith, J. "Lydgate's Changes in the *Temple of Glas*." *Medium Aevum* 27 (1958), 166–72.

Ovid. *The Art of Love and Other Poems*. Trans. J. M. Mozley; rev. G. P. Goold. Loeb Classical Library. Cambridge, MA: Harvard University Press, 1979.

———. *Fasti*. Trans. James George Frazer; rev. G. P. Goold. Loeb Classical Library. Cambridge, MA: Harvard University Press, 1989.

———. *Heroides and Amores*. Trans. Grant Showerman; rev. G. P. Goold. Loeb Classical Library. Cambridge, MA: Harvard University Press, 1977.

———. *Metamorphoses*. Trans. Frank Justus Miller; rev. G. P. Goold. 2 vols. Loeb Classical Library. Cambridge, MA: Harvard University Press, 1984.

Pearsall, Derek. *John Lydgate*. London: Routledge and Kegan Paul, 1970.

———. *John Lydgate (1371–1449): A Bio-Bibliography*. Victoria, BC: University of Victoria, 1997.

———. "Lydgate as Innovator." *Modern Language Quarterly* 53 (1992), 5–22.

The Poetical Works of Geoffrey Chaucer: A Facsimile of Cambridge University Library MS GG. 4.27. Vol. 3. Intro. M. B. Parkes and Richard Beadle. Norman, OK: Pilgrim Books, 1980.

Pollard, Alfred W., and G. R. Redgrave. *A Short-Title Catalogue of Books Printed in England, Scotland, and Ireland and of English Books Printed Abroad, 1475–1640*. Second ed., rev. and enlarged by W. A. Jackson, F. S. Ferguson, and Katharine F. Pantzer. 3 vols. London: Bibliographical Society, 1976–91.

Reimer, Stephen R. "The Canon of John Lydgate: A Progress Report." A paper presented to The International Congress on the Fifteenth Century, Kaprun bei Salzburg, July, 1995. http://www.ualberta.ca/~sreimer/proj/kaprun.htm

Renoir, Alain. "Attitudes toward Women in Lydgate's Poetry." *English Studies* 42 (1961), 1–14.

———. "The Binding Knot: Three Uses of One Image in Lydgate's Poetry." *Neophilologus* 41 (1957), 202–04.

———. *The Poetry of John Lydgate*. London: Routledge and Kegan Paul, 1967.

Renoir, Alain, and C. David Benson. "John Lydgate." In Severs, Hartung, and Biedler, vol. 6. 1980. Pp. 1809–1920 and 2071–2175.

Robbins, Rossell Hope. *Secular Lyrics of the XIV and XV Centuries*. Second ed. Oxford: Clarendon Press, 1955.

Robinson, Ian. *Chaucer's Prosody: A Study of the Middle English Verse Tradition*. Cambridge: Cambridge University Press, 1971.

Russell, J. Stephen. *The English Dream Vision: Anatomy of a Form*. Columbus: Ohio State University Press, 1988.

Scanlon, Larry. "Lydgate's Poetics: Laureation and Domesticity in the *Temple of Glass*." In Scanlon and Simpson, pp. 61-97.

Scanlon, Larry, and James Simpson, eds. *John Lydgate: Poetry, Culture, and Lancastrian England*. Notre Dame, IN: University of Notre Dame Press, 2006.

Schirmer, Walter F. *John Lydgate: A Study in the Culture of the XVth Century*. Trans. Ann E. Keep. London: Methuen, 1961.

Seaton, Ethel. *Sir Richard Roos, c. 1410–1482, Lancastrian Poet*. London: Rupert Hart-Davis, 1961.

Severs, J. Burke, Albert E. Hartung, and Peter G. Biedler, gen. eds. *A Manual of the Writings in Middle English, 1050–1500*. 11 vols. to date. New Haven: Connecticut Academy of Arts and Sciences, 1967–. [Severs is gen. ed. for vols. 1–2; Hartung is gen. ed. for vols. 3–10; Biedler is gen. ed. for vols. 11–.]

Simpson, James. *The Oxford English Literary History, Volume 2, 1350–1547: Reform and Cultural Revolution*. Oxford: Oxford University Press, 2002.

Spearing, A. C. *Medieval Dream-Poetry*. Cambridge: Cambridge University Press, 1976.

———. *Medieval to Renaissance in English Poetry*. Cambridge: Cambridge University Press, 1985.

———. *The Medieval Poet as Voyeur: Looking and Listening in Medieval Love-Narratives*. Cambridge: Cambridge University Press, 1993.

Strickland, Agnes. *Lives of the Queens of England*. Vol. 3. London: Henry Colburn, 1840.

Symons, Dana M., ed. *Chaucerian Dream Visions and Complaints*. Kalamazoo, MI: Medieval Institute Publications, 2004.

Tinkle, Theresa. *Medieval Venuses and Cupids: Sexuality, Hermeneutics, and English Poetry*. Stanford, CA: Stanford University Press, 1996.

Torti, Anna. *The Glass of Form: Mirroring Structures from Chaucer to Skelton*. Cambridge: D.S. Brewer, 1991.

Twycross, Meg. *The Medieval Anadyomene: A Study in Chaucer's Mythography*. Oxford: Basil Blackwell, 1972.

Virgil. *Vergil*. Trans. H. Rushton Fairclough; rev. G. P. Goold. 2 vols. Vol. 1: *Eclogues, Georgics, Aeneid I–VI*; Vol. 2: *Aeneid VII–XII*. Loeb Classical Library. Cambridge, MA: Harvard University Press, 1999.

Walker, Eric C. "The Muse of Indifference." *PMLA* 120 (2005), 197–218.

Whiting, Bartlett Jere, with the collaboration of Helen Wescott Whiting. *Proverbs, Sentences, and Proverbial Phrases from English Writings Mainly before 1500*. Cambridge, MA: The Belknap Press of Harvard University Press, 1968.

Wilson, Janet. "Poet and Patron in Early Fifteenth-Century England: John Lydgate's *Temple of Glas*." *Parergon* 11 (1975), 25–32.

Windeatt, B. A., ed. and trans. *Chaucer's Dream Poetry: Sources and Analogues*. Cambridge: D. S. Brewer, 1982.

GLOSSARY

abaisshed *embarrassed*
abide(th, ing) *to wait, be patient; remain*
abounde *to be abundant*
abraide *to wake, regain consciousness; start up, move*
adoun(e) *down, downward; below*
affeccioun *emotion, feeling; desire*
affray *fear, dismay; disturbance*
afore *before, previously*
againes *against, in opposition; in front of; toward*
againward *back again; in return*
agre *graciously*
akoye *to soothe*
alderlast *last of all*
aldernext *next, nearest of all*
amate *dismayed; overcome*
amende *to remedy, correct; make amends*
amyd *in the middle of*
amys *wrong, amiss*
anon(e) *at once, immediately*
apaide *pleased, satisfied*
arace *to erase; pluck out*
aspectes *bearing; looks, appearance; influence*
assautes *attacks, assaults*
assay (n.) *test, trial*
assay (v.) *to test, assay; attempt*
asswage *mitigate, relieve; lessen*
astert *to escape; slip out*
astonyed *stunned, amazed, bewildered*
atones *at once; in one body, together*
atwixen *between*
auter *altar*
avaunce *to advance*
avaunte *to boast*
axcesse *sickness*

axe *to ask; demand; require*
ay(e) *always, ever*

bataile *battle, war; hostility*
bawme *fragrance*
behest *promise*
bemes *beams, rays of light*
benigne (adj.) *gracious, kind*
benignité (n.) *good will, kindness*
benygneli (adv.) *graciously*
bere *to bear, carry*
bette *better*
betwix *between*
bie *to buy, purchase*
bihote *to promise*
bil *petition, request, prepared complaint*
bise *active, busy; diligent, attentive*
bite *to bite, cut, pierce*
bitide *to happen, occur*
bitt *to bid; request*
bole *bull*
bore *boar*
borow *guarantee, pledge*
bote *relief, remedy*
bounté (n.) *goodness, virtue; excellence; generous*
bounteous (adj.) *good, worthy*
bowghis *boughs*
brenne *to burn*
brid *bird*
bridel *bridle*
bronte *to rush*
buxumnes *obedience, humility*

caas *situation; event; chance; action*
causeles *without reason, cause*
celestial *heavenly*

91

champartie *dispute, litigation*
clepe *to call*
compassid *to be enclosed, contained;*
  plan, plot
connyng *skill*
contune *to continue*
corage *nature, make-up; heart, spirit*
couthe *known, familiar; renowned*
covetise *covetousness*
curtesie *courtesy, courtliness*

daister *morning star, luminary*
daliaunce *sociable conversation*
daunt(e) *to subdue, compel*
defaute *lack, absence; fault*
defence *resistance, hindrance*
deie(n) *to die*
deinté *excellent, pleasing*
demening *demeanor*
demeyned *controlled, guided*
depured *purified*
dere *dear, excellent; expensive*
descriven *to describe, tell about*
dessever(e) *to separate*
devoid(e) *lacking*
devoider *dispeller*
dilacioun *delay*
discure *to tell, disclose; uncover*
dispitous *contemptuous, merciless*
dole *grief, pain*
doleful *sad, mournful*
dome *judgment; decision; opinion*
donne (adj.) *dark, dusky; lowering*
donne (v.) *to fade, darken*
dueté *duty; matter of obligation*
dures *force; harshness*

eeke *also*
eft(e) *again; after, then*
embrouded *embroidered*
emprise *enterprise; purpose; power*
endite *to write, compose; describe*
enlumynd *illuminated*
ennuyd *colored; ornamented*
entaile (n.) *art of sculpture; form,*
  appearance
entaile (v.) *to carve, sculpt; decorate*

ententif *eager; attentive*
entere *perfect; sincere, devoted; beloved,*
  dear
enviroun *all around*
estres *location, area; building;*
  circumstances
evenlich *evenly, equally*
everedel (adv.) *wholly, completely*
everedele (n.) *everything*
everich *each*
ewrous *prosperous, successful; fortunate;*
  happy

feine *to pretend, feign*
ferforth(e) *insofar, to the extent*
ferse *fierce*
ferther *further*
fervence *heat; ardor*
fest *feast*
flitten *to flee; remove*
forcasteth *casts forth; overthrows*
fordrive *tossed about*
forthbi *past; alongside; near*
forwrynkled *twisted, convoluted,*
  enfolded
fro *from; away from*
fyne (1) *to end, cease*
fyne (2) *to refine, purify*

gal *bile; bitterness*
gan *began*
gentilles *nobility*
gie *lead, guide; advise; rule*
ginneth *begins*
gise *behavior, manner*
glade(st, ing) (v.) *to gladden, comfort*
gladsome *cheerful; cheering*
godhode *godhead, divinity; virtue*
goodeli (adj.) *excellent, beautiful,*
  pleasurable
goodeli (adv.) *excellently, graciously*
goodlihed (n.) *excellence, virtue, beauty*
gre *graciously, without complaint*
grettir *greater*
grove *grove*
grucch(-ing) *to complain, rebel, begrudge*

guerdon (n.) *reward, requital*
guerdone (v.) *to reward, requite*

habound *to be full, plentiful; overflow*
halowe *to hallow, consecrate; worship, celebrate*
hard(e) *firm; difficult; cruel*
hardi *bold, daring*
hardines *boldness*
hatter *hotter*
hauteyn *haughty, proud*
hede *heed, attention*
hem *them*
hennes *hence*
her, hir(e) *her; their*
here *here*
here(n) *to hear*
hest(is) *vow*
hit *it*
homagere *servant*
hwe *color, complexion; appearance*

ich(e) *each*
ifrore *to be frozen*
iliche *in like manner; constantly*
iouth *youth*
ipersid *pierced, penetrated*
ire *anger*

jewise *punishment; torment; judgment*
jocond *cheerful, lighthearted*

kalendes *first day of the month; beginning; harbinger*
kouthe *known, familiar*
kunnyng *knowledge; skill; cunning*
kynd(e) *nature*

laiser *opportune time; leisure time; respite*
lase *cord, snare*
laude *acclaim, praise*
lech *physician*
ledne *language; birdsong*
lere *to learn; teach*
levyr *rather; more desirable*
licour *juice, liquid*
lisse *assuage, lessen*

list *to desire; be pleased; choose*
lith(e) *lies, resides*
louli (adj.) *humble, modest*
louli (adv.) *humbly, modestly*
loureth *scowls*
lowlihed *humility*
lust *desire, will; pleasure; inclination*
lusti *pleasing; eager, vigorous; amorous*
lustines *pleasure; vigor*

maseth *bewilders, amazes*
mede *profit; reward; compensation*
menes *means, intermediaries*
meve *to move*
mot *must*
myne *to undermine; break into*
myschef(e) *trouble, misfortune; misconduct*
mysty *misty, full of fog; obscure; portentous*

neigh(eth) *to approach, come nearer*
nold *would not, did not want*
non *no*
no(o)n *none*
nufangilnes *novelty*
nygh *near, close to*
nyl *will not, do not wish to*
nys *is not*
nyst *knew not, did not know*

obeissaunce *homage, act of obedience, submission*
offencioun *sin, transgression*
on *on; upon; in*
onys *once*
o(o)n *one*
o(o)nli *only; exclusively; specially*
oratorie *chapel; place for prayer*
orisoun *prayer, act of praying; petitioning*
overdrawe *to pass away; spread across*
overgon(e) *to overcome; pass away*
overpace *to skip over*

pantire *bird trap, snare*
passeth *passes, proceeds; surpasses, excels*
pauper *paper*

peinte *to depict, paint, write*
peping *piping, crying*
peraventure *perhaps, by chance*
percaas *perhaps, by chance; as fate would have it*
perre *jewel, pearl*
persant *sharp, penetrating*
peté *pity, tenderness; piety*
plein *to complain*
pore *the poor*
port *demeanor, manner*
possid *thrust, tossed*
prefe *proof; experience*
pres(e) *crowd*
presscience *prescience, providence*
pris (n.) *price, value; praise; honor*
pris (v.) *to appraise, estimate; prize*
priveli *secretly*
privete *privacy, secrecy; secret counsel*
processe *narrative, discourse*
purveaunce *foresight*
purvey *to foresee; prepare*

queme *to gratify*
quite *to requite, repay, reward*

ravysshid *seized, carried away; enraptured*
recch *to care*
recounford *consolation, comfort*
recured *recovered*
rede *council; remedy; plan*
regalie *royalty*
rekeles *reckless, negligent*
reken *to consider*
remue *to prevent; alter; vary*
remyssyoun *release, grant of freedom*
reneye *to renounce*
reuthe *pity, compassion*
rife *pierce, split, divide*
rithes *rites*
rodi *reddish*
rolles *scrolls*
rotid *rooted, fixed, established*
rought(e) *cared*
rwe *to be sorry, have pity, sympathize*

sad(de) *serious, sober; steadfast; trustworthy*
salve *medicine; relief*
sate *sat*
sauf *secure, safe*
sease *seize*
sech(en) *to seek, look about; beseech*
semelines *attractiveness*
seth *sees*
shene *bright*
shew(e) *show, reveal, uncover*
sikirnes *security; certainty*
sith(en) *since; next, then; afterward*
skil *reason; reasonable*
slough *killed*
socoure *aid; protection; refuge*
sole *solitary, alone*
solein *solitary*
somwhile *sometimes, for a specified time*
sondri *sundry, various*
sote *sweet*
soth(e) *truth*
sothefast *true, genuine, authentic*
sowne *sound*
spill *to kill*
sterve *to die*
stoneith *stuns, befuddles*
sue *to follow, pursue*
sufferaunce *patience, long-suffering*
suffisaunce *sufficiency*
sureté *warranty, security*
surmounteth *surpasses*

tarie *to delay, waste time*
thou *you*
toforn(e) *before, ahead*
transmwe *to transform; alter*
tretis *treatise; document; literary work*
tristesse *melancholy, distress, despair*
tristi *faithful, secure*
trow *to believe, trust*

unnethe *scarcely, hardly; with difficulty*
unwarli *unexpectedly, unawares; suddenly*
uppermore *up higher; uppermost*

vaileth *to be beneficial, value; prevail*
vaunte *to boast*
verrai *genuine, true*
viage *journey; undertaking*
visitacioun *act of visiting; manifesting*
voide *to expel, remove; empty; nullify*

wan *sickly*
wanhope *despair*
waped *draped, covered; overcome*
wawe *wave*
weke *weak*
welbesein *nice-looking, attractive*
wel(e) (adv.) *well; very much; fully*
wele (n.) *weal, well-being; happiness; wellspring*

were (n.) *state of doubt, distress; wire*
werre *war, battle*
wex(in) *to grow, increase*
weymentacioun *lamentation*
weyve *to turn aside*
whilom *formerly, once*
willi *willing; wily, crafty*
wise *way, manner*
wisse *to guide, rule*
wit(en) *to know, learn*
woid *vowed*
wreke *to be revenged*
wrought *to work, make*

ye *you*
yeve(n) *to give*
yold(e) *made to yield, render; captured*

MIDDLE ENGLISH TEXTS SERIES

The Trials and Joys of Marriage, edited by Eve Salisbury (2002)

Middle English Legends of Women Saints, edited by Sherry L. Reames, with assistance of Martha G. Blalock and Wendy R. Larson (2003)

The Wallace: Selections, edited by Anne McKim (2003)

Richard Maidstone, *Concordia (The Reconciliation of Richard II with London)*, edited by David R. Carlson, with a verse translation by A. G. Rigg (2003)

Three Purgatory Poems: The Gast of Gy, Sir Owain, The Vision of Tundale, edited by Edward E. Foster (2004)

William Dunbar, *The Complete Works*, edited by John Conlee (2004)

Chaucerian Dream Visions and Complaints, edited by Dana M. Symons (2004)

Stanzaic Guy of Warwick, edited by Alison Wiggins (2004)

Saints' Lives in Middle English Collections, edited by E. Gordon Whatley, with Anne B. Thompson and Robert K. Upchurch (2004)

Siege of Jerusalem, edited by Michael Livingston (2004)

The Kingis Quair and Other Prison Poems, edited by Linne R. Mooney and Mary-Jo Arn (2005)

Chaucerian Apocrypha: Selections, edited by Kathleen Forni (2005)

John Gower, *The Minor Latin Works*, edited and translated by R. F. Yeager, with *In Praise of Peace*, edited by Michael Livingston (2005)

Sentimental and Humorous Romances: Floris and Blancheflour, Sir Degrevant, The Squire of Low Degree, The Tournament of Tottenham, and The Feast of Tottenham, edited by Erik Kooper (2006)

The Dicts and Sayings of the Philosophers, edited by John William Sutton (2006)

Everyman and Its Dutch Original, Elckerlijc, edited by Clifford Davidson, Martin W. Walsh, and Ton J. Broos (2006)

The N-Town Plays, edited by Douglas Sugano, with assistance by Victor I. Scherb (2007)

The Book of John Mandeville, edited by Tamarah Kohanski and C. David Benson (2007)

DOCUMENTS OF PRACTICE SERIES

Love and Marriage in Late Medieval London, selected, translated, and introduced by Shannon McSheffrey (1995)

Sources for the History of Medicine in Late Medieval England, selected, introduced, and translated by Carole Rawcliffe (1995)

A Slice of Life: Selected Documents of Medieval English Peasant Experience, edited, translated, and with an introduction by Edwin Brezette DeWindt (1996)

Regular Life: Monastic, Canonical, and Mendicant Rules, selected and introduced by Douglas J. McMillan and Kathryn Smith Fladenmuller (1997); second edition, selected and introduced by Daniel Marcel La Corte and Douglas J. McMillan (2004)

Women and Monasticism in Medieval Europe: Sisters and Patrons of the Cistercian Reform, selected, translated, and with an introduction by Constance H. Berman (2002)

Medieval Notaries and Their Acts: The 1327–1328 Register of Jean Holanie, introduced, edited, and translated by Kathryn L. Reyerson and Debra A. Salata (2004)

COMMENTARY SERIES

Haimo of Auxerre, *Commentary on the Book of Jonah*, translated with an introduction and notes by Deborah Everhart (1993)

Medieval Exegesis in Translation: Commentaries on the Book of Ruth, translated with an introduction and notes by Lesley Smith (1996)

Nicholas of Lyra's Apocalypse Commentary, translated with an introduction and notes by Philip D. W. Krey (1997)

Rabbi Ezra Ben Solomon of Gerona, *Commentary on the Song of Songs and Other Kabbalistic Commentaries*, selected, translated, and annotated by Seth Brody (1999)

John Wyclif, *On the Truth of Holy Scripture*, translated with an introduction and notes by Ian Christopher Levy (2001)

Second Thessalonians: Two Early Medieval Apocalyptic Commentaries, introduced and translated by Steven R. Cartwright and Kevin L. Hughes (2001)

The Glossa Ordinaria on the Song of Songs, translated with an introduction and notes by Mary Dove (2004)

MEDIEVAL GERMAN TEXTS IN BILINGUAL EDITIONS SERIES

Sovereignty and Salvation in the Vernacular, 1050–1150, introduction, translations, and notes by James A. Schultz (2000)

Ava's New Testament Narratives: "When the Old Law Passed Away," introduction, translation, and notes by James A. Rushing, Jr. (2003)

History as Literature: German World Chronicles of the Thirteenth Century in Verse, introduction, translation, and notes by R. Graeme Dunphy (2003)

VARIA

The Study of Chivalry: Resources and Approaches, edited by Howell Chickering and Thomas H. Seiler (1988)

Studies in the Harley Manuscript: The Scribes, Contents, and Social Contexts of British Library MS Harley 2253, edited by Susanna Fein (2000)

The Liturgy of the Medieval Church, edited by Thomas J. Heffernan and E. Ann Matter (2001; second edition 2005)

TO ORDER PLEASE CONTACT:

Medieval Institute Publications
Western Michigan University
Kalamazoo, MI 49008-5432
Phone (269) 387-8755
FAX (269) 387-8750

http://www.wmich.edu/medieval/mip/index.html

Medieval Institute Publications is a program
of The Medieval Institute, College of Arts
and Sciences, Western Michigan University

Typeset in 10/13 New Baskerville
with Golden Cockerel Ornaments display
Designed by Linda K. Judy
Manufactured by Cushing-Malloy, Inc.

Medieval Institute Publications
College of Arts and Sciences
Western Michigan University
1903 W. Michigan Avenue
Kalamazoo, MI 49008-5432
http://www.wmich.edu/medieval/mip

 WESTERN MICHIGAN UNIVERSITY